Has Psalm 156 Been Found?

"It is scarcely an exaggeration to say that Princeton Theological Seminary Professor James H. Charlesworth plays the role of a contemporary Indiana Jones. In this fascinating book he shows persuasively that the Hebrew text MS RNL Antonin 798, recovered in the nineteenth century from the Cairo synagogue genizah, in all likelihood preserves an authentic pre-70 CE psalm, which in the pre-Christian era was believed to be a psalm of David."
—CRAIG A. EVANS, Houston Theological Seminary

"Charlesworth offers here a detailed, clearly argued, and provocative analysis of a little-known text, which he proposes should be considered 'Psalm 156'. He also shows how his proposed identification and dating of the text has relevance for the study of ancient Judaism and early Christianity."
—LARRY HURTADO, University of Edinburgh

"Charlesworth offers a careful translation and well-informed analysis of primary and secondary sources surrounding this important but often ignored ancient text that is almost the size of Psalm 119. He argues for an early origin of Psalm 156, around 100 BCE, and its history from the Judean desert to the Cairo Genizah and finally to the St. Petersburgh Library (MS RNL Antonin 798). Scholars interested in the complex history and interpretation of this ancient text cannot ignore this carefully prepared investigation."
—LEE MARTIN MCDONALD, Acadia University

"Professor Charlesworth, one of the most eminent scholars in the Dead Sea Scrolls, suggests that in a medieval manuscript from the Cairo Geniza a psalm of David is preserved showing close relations to the extra-Biblical Psalms 151–155; he therefore proposes to label it Ps 156. A translation, aiming to reflect the poetry of the Hebrew psalms, and a commentary are the center of this fine book."
—HERMANN LICHTENBERGER, University of Tübingen

"James Charlesworth offers a fresh translation of the richly resonating Hebrew religious poetry contained in a single medieval manuscript, and a bold proposal concerning its connection to the Bible and to the Dead Sea Scrolls. This helpful volume provides any reader easy access to the evidence for the serious consideration his argument deserves. Charlesworth adds value to a fascinating conversation taking place in current scholarship on early Jewish psalmic writings."

—WILLIAM YARCHIN, Azusa Pacific University

Has Psalm 156 Been Found?

With Images of MS RNL Antonin 798

James H. Charlesworth

With the assistance of
BRANDON L. ALLEN

CASCADE *Books* • Eugene, Oregon

HAS PSALM 156 BEEN FOUND?
With Images of MS RNL Antonin 798

Copyright © 2018 James H. Charlesworth. All rights reserved. Except for brief quotations in critical publications or reviews, no part of this book may be reproduced in any manner without prior written permission from the publisher. Write: Permissions, Wipf and Stock Publishers, 199 W. 8th Ave., Suite 3, Eugene, OR 97401.

Cascade Books
An Imprint of Wipf and Stock Publishers
199 W. 8th Ave., Suite 3
Eugene, OR 97401

www.wipfandstock.com

PAPERBACK ISBN: 978-1-5326-4239-5
HARDCOVER ISBN: 978-1-5326-4240-1
EBOOK ISBN: 978-1-5326-4241-8

Cataloguing-in-Publication data:

Names: Charlesworth, James H., author. | Allen, Brandon Lee, assistant.

Title: Has Psalm 156 been found? : with images of MS RNL Antonin 798 / James H. Charlesworth, with the assistance of Brandon L. Allen.

Description: Eugene, OR: Cascade Books, 2018. | Includes bibliographical references.

Identifiers: ISBN: 978-1-5326-4239-5 (paperback). | ISBN: 978-1-5326-4240-1 (hardcover). | ISBN: 978-1-5326-4241-8 (epub).

Subjects: LCSH: Dead Sea Scrolls. | Bible. Psalms. Dead Sea Scrolls Psalms Scroll. | Cairo Genizah.

Classification: BS1430 C44 2018 (print). | BS1430 (epub).

Manufactured in the U.S.A.

Scripture quotations marked (NRSV) are taken from New Revised Standard Version Bible, copyright © 1989 National Council of the Churches of Christ in the United States of America. Used by permission. All rights reserved worldwide.

Scripture quotations marked (JPS TANAKH) are reprinted from *Tanakh: The New JPS Translation according to the Traditional Hebrew Text.* Copyright © 1985, 1999 by The Jewish Publication Society with the permission of the publisher.

Contents

Preface | *ix*

Abbreviations | *xi*

1. Introductions and Translations of Psalms 151–155 | 1

2. Translation of MS RNL Antonin 798 | 27

3. Has Psalm 156 Been Found? | 56

4. The Importance of Psalm 156 for the Hebrew Bible, Early Judaism, and Christianity | 77

Conclusion | 95

Appendix 1: On Beatitudes | 97

Appendix 2: Images and Transcription of MS RNL Antonin 798 | 101

Bibliography | 111

Author Index | 135

Ancient Sources Index | 137

Preface

As I shall explain in the following pages, around 800 CE Jews from Jerusalem recovered two hundred ancient manuscripts from a place "near Jericho." What place could be indicated? In the late 1940s and 1950s Bedouin and scholars found the Dead Sea Scrolls in caves near a ruin called "Qumran"; it is not far from Jericho. Thus, leading scholars rightly perceive the much earlier geographical description aptly suits the Qumran caves. The eleven Qumran caves that produced scrolls once contained well over one thousand Jewish manuscripts. The manuscripts found by medieval Jews preserved two hundred Psalms of David; yet, only 150 psalms were collected by Rabbis into the Hebrew Bible. The present monograph focuses on a virtually unknown psalm thought to be composed by David according to early Jews. Could it be one of the two hundred Psalms found in 800? You will find my search for an answer in the following chapters.

The Hebrew Bible is trifurcated into Torah, Prophets, and Writings. The third section of the canon of the Hebrew Bible, the Writings in which the Davidic Psalter is included, was not closed until long after 70 CE, when Jerusalem and the Temple were destroyed by Roman soldiers. Before 70 CE, the Davidic Psalter was not well defined, as we know clearly from the Qumran Psalms Scroll. During the time of Hillel and Jesus, the order and content of the Psalter was not established, and some psalms attributed to David were not included. Among these "Davidic Psalms" are Psalms 151–155, well known by biblical scholars, and what has not yet been numbered, and may be, Psalm 156.

Abbreviations

Modern Works

ABAJU	Arbeiten zur Geschichte des antiken Judentums und des Urchristentums
ABD	*The Anchor Bible Dictionary*
ABRL	Anchor Bible Reference Library
ALUOS	*Annual of Leeds University Oriental Society*
AT	*Acta Theologica*
ATANT	*Arbeiten zu Text und Sprache im Alten Testament*
AusBR	*Australian Biblical Review*
BASOR	*Bulletin of the American Schools of Oriental Research*
BETL	Bibliotheca Ephemridum Theologicarum Lovaniensium
BHH	*Biblisch-Historisches Handwörterbuch*
Bib	*Biblica*
BIFAO	*Bulletin de l'Institut franáais d'archéologie orientale*
BIS	Biblical Interpretation Series

Abbreviations

BJRL	*Bulletin of the John Rylands University of Manchester*
BZ	*Biblische Zeitschrift*
BZAW	Beihefte zur *Zeitschrift für die alttestamentliche Wissenschaft*
CB	*Cultura biblica*
CBQ	*Catholic Biblical Quarterly*
CRAIBL	*Cromptes rendus de l'Académie des inscriptions et belles-lettres*
CRINT	Compendia Rerum Iudaicarum ad Novum Testamentum
DJD	Discoveries in the Judean Desert
DSD	*Dead Sea Discoveries*
EncyDSS	*Encyclopedia of the Dead Sea Scrolls*
EncyJud	*Encycopaedia Judaica*
EstBib	*Estudios biblicos*
GOFS	Göttinger Orientforschungen
HSM	Harvard Semitic Monographs
HSS	Harvard Semitic Studies
HTR	*Harvard Theological Review*
HUCA	*Hebrew Union College Annual*
IEJ	*Israel Exploration Journal*
JAJSup	Journal of Ancient Judaism Supplements
JBL	*Journal of Biblical Literature*
JBLMS	Journal of Biblical Literature Monograph Series
JESOT	*Journal for the Evangelical Study of the Old Testament*

Abbreviations

JJS	Journal of Jewish Studies
JNSL	Journal of Northwest Semitic Languages
JQR	Jewish Quarterly Review
JSem	Journal for Semitics
JSHRZ	Jüdische Schriften aus hellenistisch-römischer Zeit
JSOTSup	Journal for the Study of the Old Testament Supplement Series
JSP	Journal for the Study of the Pseudepigrapha
JSS	Journal of Semitic Studies
LTP	Laval théologique et philosophique
McCQ	McCormick Quarterly
MdB	Le Monde de la Bible
NTL	New Testament Library
NTOA	Novum Testamentum et Orbis Antiquus
OTP	Old Testament Pseudepigrapha
PTSDSSP	Princeton Theological Seminary Dead Sea Scrolls Project
RHPR	Revue d'histoire et de philosophie religieuses
RHR	Revue de l'histoire des religions
RivB	Rivista biblica italiana
RQ	Revue de Qumrân
RSO	Rivista degli studi orientali
RTK	Roczniki teologiczne
SBB	Stuttgarter biblische Beiträge

ABBREVIATIONS

SBLDS	Society of Biblical Literature Dissertation Series
SBLEJL	Society of Biblical Literature Early Judaism and Its Literature
SBLSBS	Society of Biblical Literature Sources for Biblical Study
SBLSCS	Society of Biblical Literature Septuagint and Cognate Studies Series
SBLTT	Society of Biblical Literature Texts in Translation
SBS	Stuttgarter Bibelstudien
Sem	*Semitica*
SK	*Skrif en Kerk*
SJ	Studia Judaica
SNTSMS	Society for New Testament Studies Monograph Series
STDJ	Studies on the Text of the Desert of Judah
TLZ	*Theologische Literaturzeitung*
TWQ	*Theologisches Wörterbuch zu de Qumrantexten*
VT	*Vetus Testamentum*
VTSup	Vetus Testamentum Supplements
WTJ	*Westminster Theological Journal*
ZAW	*Zeitschrift für die alttestamentliche Wissenschaft*
ZDMG	*Zeitschrift der deutschen morgenländischen Gesellschaft*

Scripture Abbreviations

Hebrew Bible / Old Testament

Gen	Judg	Neh	Song	Hos	Nah
Exod	Ruth	Esth	Isa	Joel	Hab
Lev	1–2 Sam	Job	Jer	Amos	Zeph
Num	1–2 Kgs	Ps (*pl.* Pss)	Lam	Obad	Hag
Deut	1–2 Chr	Prov	Ezek	Jonah	Zech
Josh	Ezra	Eccl	Dan	Mic	Mal

New Testament

Matt	Acts	Eph	1–2 Tim	Heb	1–2–3 John
Mark	Rom	Phil	Titus	Jas	Jude
Luke	1–2 Cor	Col	Phlm	1–2 Pet	Rev
John	Gal	1–2 Thess			

Apocryphal / Deuterocanonical Books

Tob	Wis	1–3 Esd	Sg Three	Bel	3–4 Macc
Jdt	Sir	Ep Jer	Sus	1–2 Macc	Pr Man
Add Esth		Bar			

Pseudepigrapha and Other Ancient Sources

ActsPaul	*Acts of Paul*
Ant.	Josephus, *Antiquities of the Jews*
1En	*1 Enoch*
2En	*2 Enoch*
Gos. Thom.	*Gospel of Thomas*
HistRech	*History of the Rechabites*
LAB	*Liber Antiquitatum Biblicarum*

Abbreviations

NH	Pliny the Elder, *Naturalis Historia*
OdesSol	*Odes of Solomon*
Ps-Philo	*Pseudo-Philo*
PssSol	*Psalms of Solomon*
TgIsa	*Targum of Isaiah*
War	Josephus, *Wars of the Jews*

1

Introductions and Translations of Psalms 151–155

Introduction

Jews and Christians who read the Bible cherish the 150 Psalms included in the Davidic Psalter.[1] Due to the discoveries of ancient and medieval manuscripts and studies of the Greek and Syriac versions of the so-called Old Testament, we now know of 155 and perhaps 156 Psalms of David.[2] Psalm 151 is preserved in Greek, Hebrew, Syriac, Latin, Coptic, Ethiopic, Armenian, and Arabic.

---

1. The major commentaries on the Davidic Psalter are too numerous to list. They can be found under "Psalms" in most theological libraries. The recent commentaries or major studies on the Psalter that I found insightful, informed, and critical are by the following biblical savants (knowing the name of the author makes it easy to find the commentary in a major library): Westermann (1980, 1981, 1989), James Kugel (1981), Gerald H. Wilson (1985), Patrick D. Miller (1986), Hans-Joachim Kraus (1986, 1988, 1989), F. W. Dobbs-Allsopp (2015 [also see his replete bibliography on pp. 525–63]).

2. I am now exploring if Psalm 156 has been found. For the best work on Psalms 151–155, see Charlesworth with Sanders, "More Psalms of David," 609–24; Sanders, *The Psalms Scroll of Qumran Cave 11*; Sanders, *The Dead Sea Psalms Scroll*; Baars, "Apocryphal Psalms."

Psalms 152 and 153 are known only in Syriac. Psalms 154 and 155 are extant in Hebrew and Syriac. What seems to be Psalm 156 is preserved only in one medieval Hebrew manuscript. The Hebrew manuscripts of these psalms are earlier and most likely in the original language; a lost Hebrew text may lie behind all the other psalms.[3]

These Non-Masoretic Psalms are collected after the 150 Davidic Psalms in the twelfth-century Syriac Davidic Psalter as well as in Bishop Elijah's tenth-century *The Book of Discipline*. The importance of these psalms became obvious when Psalms 151, 154, and 155 were found in the Qumran *Psalms Scroll*.[4] At least these three psalms, and probably all of them, antedate 70 CE. Their postexilic date seems confirmed by the Hebrew style and language as well as the citations or echoes of earlier biblical books (see notes to the translation).

Psalms 151 A and B

The original language of Psalm 151, actually portions of two psalms (Psalms 151 A and B), is Hebrew. The Syriac of Psalms 151 A and B derives from and is dependent upon the Greek tradition (LXX), but a Hebrew original looms likely. In contrast, the Syriac of Psalms 152–155 most likely comes directly from the Hebrew.[5]

A comparison of the Syriac and Hebrew of Psalms 151–155 reveals that the Syriac of 151 A and 151 B, in contrast to Psalms 154 and 155, is dissimilar to the Hebrew. Originally Psalm 151 was

---

3. The Hebrew (when it is extant) and the parallel Greek and Syriac texts, with translations and notes, are found in Charlesworth et al., "Non-Masoretic Psalms," 155–215. Also see the earlier translations of Psalms 151–155 with notes in Charlesworth and Sanders, "More Psalms of David," 609–24.

4. See Sanders, *The Psalms Scroll of Qumrân*; and Pigué, *The Syriac Apocryphal Psalms*. Very helpful are the comments in Pigué, "Psalms, Syriac (Apocryphal)," 536–37.

5. See Strugnell, "Notes on the Text," 278. In "Les Textes grec et syriaque du Psaume 151," 548–64, Jean Magne failed to refute Strugnell's arguments and mistakenly thought that the Syriac and Greek of 151 are "two independent versions of the Hebrew."

two separate Psalms (151 A and 151 B); unfortunately, most of the Hebrew text of 151 B is lost because it is preserved only in the Qumran *Psalms Scroll*, and this section of 11QPs^a is worn away. It seems odd that the Greek (LXX) and Syriac also have truncated versions of both psalms.

Psalms 151 A and 151 B predate the second century BCE. The combined psalms are in the Greek Septuagint, which antedates that period. Frank Moore Cross correctly argued that the collected psalm cannot "be later than the 3rd century B.C."[6] S. Piqué opines that Psalm 151 A "could be dated to the 6th century B.C.E., or earlier, on stylistic grounds; but it contains certain phrases which suggest a later date."[7] This early date certainly dismisses the possibility that Psalm 151 was composed by Hasmonean priests or at Qumran, since the Essenes were not at Qumran until sometime after the middle of the second century BCE, at the earliest.[8]

In the Syriac recension, an interpolation is found in v. 2: "And I discovered a lion and a wolf and I killed and rent them." The idea is intrusive to the thought of the psalm, is not preserved in 11QPs^a (11Q5), is only in the margin of MS A (which is the most reliable Syriac tradition), and is missing in JRL Syr. 7. The line has been interpolated from Psalms 152 and 153 and is an echo of Ps 17:36–38.

151 A (11QPs^a 151 = 11Q5)

Translated from the Hebrew

A Hallelujah of David the Son of Jesse

151 A

And among my brothers, I was the smallest,
   And the youngest among the sons of my father.

---

6. Cross, "David, Orpheus, and Psalm 151:3–4," 70.
7. Pigué, "Psalms, Syriac (Apocryphal)," 537.
8. Charlesworth, *The Pesharim and Qumran History*.

And he (God) made me shepherd of his flocks,
And the ruler over his kids.[9]

2 My hands made a flute,
And my fingers a lyre.

And I shall render glory to the Lord,[10]
I thought within myself.[11]

3 The mountains cannot witness to him,
Nor the hills proclaim (him).

The trees have elevated my words,
And the flocks my deeds.[12]

4 For who can proclaim and who can announce,
And who can recount the deeds of the Lord?

Everything God has seen;
Everything he has heard and he has listened.

5 He sent his prophet to anoint me,
Samuel to make me great.

---

9. The author of the *Hymn of the Pearl* probably knew this psalm (vs. 1): "When I was a little lad / And dwelling in my kingdom, the house of my father ..." (trans. Charlesworth).

10. In this psalm God is "the Lord God" (see v. 6).

11. Or "in my soul."

12. Numerous translations have been defended; see Sanders *The Dead Sea Psalms Scroll*, 100–103. Strugnell ("Notes on the Text," 280) renders this verse as follows: "The mountains cannot witness to Him / nor the hills proclaim about Him / (Nor) the trees (proclaim) His words / nor the flocks His deeds." For a thoroughly different translation, see Magne, "Orphisme, pythagorisme, essénisme dans le texte hébreu du Psaume 151?" 508–47, see especially p. 532 (and 544). See also, Carmignac, "Nouvelles Precisions sur le Psaume 151," 593–97.

My brothers went out to meet him,
Handsome of figure and handsome of appearance.

6 (Although) their stature was tall,
(And) their hair handsome,
The Lord God
Never choose them.

7 But he sent and took me from behind the flock,
And he anointed me with holy oil,
And he made me leader for his people,
And ruler over the sons of his covenant.

Notice the refined poetry in Psalm 151 A mirrors the Davidic Psalter; it also seems edited. The thought appears in two, and then four, parallel lines of thought. The second line has terms and concepts that are synonymous with the first line; thus, "the smallest" is followed by "the youngest" and "shepherd" is defined as "ruler." Then "a flute" is parallel to "a lyre." In v. 3 "the mountains" are similar to "the hills" and the interrogative "who can proclaim" is followed by "who can recount." In v. 5 "his prophet" is specified as the prophet "Samuel" who anointed David and made him great. In the final verse, David is "anointed" and becomes "leader" and "ruler." The parallel poetry is, as F. W. Dobbs-Allsopp states, "the best known and best understood feature of biblical verses."[13] The Professor of Poetry at Oxford, Robert Lowth, composed a groundbreaking book called *De Sacra Poesi Hebraeorum* which contains lectures presented between 1741 and 1751.[14] In it he observed that Hebrew poetry is presented as *parallelismus membrorum* in which thought is organized in two (or more) lines in which, as if according to "a kind of rule or measure," thoughts and words are presented in parallel lines (often lost to view because Hebrew manuscripts are arranged in columns and lines oblivious of poetic style). Yet

---

13. Dobbs-Allsopp, *On Biblical* Poetry, 3.
14. Lowth, *De Sacra Poesi Hebraeorum*. See now Lowth, *The Major Works*, edited by David A. Reibel.

parallelism is not the only feature, as the leading experts on biblical poetry have stressed for centuries. One of the distinctive features of Hebrew poetry is not rhyme or meter but rhythm; however, it is virtually impossible to convey rhythm in translation.[15]

151 B (11QPs[a] 151)

Translated from the Hebrew

At the Beginning of [Dav]id's Po[w]er

After the Prophet of God Anointed Him[16]

1 Then I s[a]w a Philistine
  Who was uttering taunts from the ra[nks of the enemy . . .]

  I [. . .] the [. . .]

151 B (5ApocSyrPs 1b)

Translated from the Syriac

(Text is continuous with 151 A:1–5 in Syriac)

1 I went out to attack the Philistine,
  And he cursed me by his idols.

2 But after I unsheathed his sword, I cut off his head;
  And I removed the shame from the sons of Israel.

---

15. See Dobbs-Allsopp, *On Biblical Poetry*, 99 [and chapter 2].

16. 11QPs[a] 151 preserves two psalms, 151 A and 151 B. These two psalms were truncated in the Greek (LXX) and Syriac. Strugnell warns that it is "uncertain whether this secondary text [151 B] ever existed in Hebrew" ("Notes on the Text and Transmission," 259). Plate 17 (in Sanders, *The Psalm Scroll*) shows, however, that a portion of it is preserved in 11QPs[a]; the manuscript is severely damaged at this place, yet lines 13 and 14 are clearly extant.

Introductions and Translations of Psalms 151–155

Attribution to David of Psalms 151 A and 151 B.

Psalms 151 A and 151 B are obviously composed in honor of David. The inscription to Psalm 151 A in Hebrew, Greek [LXX], and the Peshiṭta stipulates that the psalm was composed by David. Note the Greek: "This psalm (is) truly written by David, though supernumery, when he singlehandedly fought Goliath." Passages in 1 Samuel are echoed in Psalm 151 A and B. Psalm 151 A is influenced by 1 Sam 16:6–13; here is the story:

> **6** When they came, he looked on Eliab and thought, "Surely the LORD's anointed is now before the LORD." **7** But the LORD said to Samuel, "Do not look on his appearance or on the height of his stature, because I have rejected him; for the LORD does not see as mortals see; they look on the outward appearance, but the LORD looks on the heart." **8** Then Jesse called Abinadab, and made him pass before Samuel. He said, "Neither has the LORD chosen this one." **9** Then Jesse made Shammah pass by. And he said, "Neither has the LORD chosen this one." **10** Jesse made seven of his sons pass before Samuel, and Samuel said to Jesse, "The LORD has not chosen any of these." **11** Samuel said to Jesse, "Are all your sons here?" And he said, "There remains yet the youngest, but he is keeping the sheep." And Samuel said to Jesse, "Send and bring him; for we will not sit down until he comes here." **12** He sent and brought him in. Now he was ruddy, and had beautiful eyes, and was handsome. The LORD said, "Rise and anoint him; for this is the one." **13** Then Samuel took the horn of oil, and anointed him in the presence of his brothers; and the spirit of the LORD came mightily upon David from that day forward. [NRSV]

Psalm 151 A does refer in line 8 (only in Hebrew; 11Q5 col. 28), in line 11 (in Hebrew; see also line 13) and verse 4c (in Greek and Syriac) to David as "anointed" (in Hebrew by Samuel, the prophet). Conspicuously absent are any clear messianic claims. Many experts will conclude that Psalm 151 antedates the belief in an eschatological and apocalyptic figure who will come as "the Messiah," or "the Anointed One." The belief in a cosmic Messiah who will bring an end to all normal history is usually dated in the history of Early Judaism to about 100 BCE.[17]

Psalm 151 B is shaped by the story of how David defeated Goliath, according to 1 Samuel 17. Here is that story:

> Now the Philistines gathered their armies for battle; they were gathered at Socoh . . . **2** Saul and the Israelites gathered and encamped in the valley of Elah, and formed ranks against the Philistines. **3** The Philistines stood on the mountain on the one side, and Israel stood on the mountain on the other side, with a valley between them.
>
> **4** And there came out from the camp of the Philistines a champion named Goliath, of Gath, whose height was six cubits and a span. **5** He had a helmet of bronze on his head, and he was armed with a coat of mail; the weight of the coat was five thousand shekels of bronze. **6** He had greaves of bronze on his legs and a javelin of bronze slung between his shoulders. **7** The shaft of his spear was like a weaver's beam, and his spear's head weighed six hundred shekels of iron; and his shield-bearer went before him. **8** He stood and shouted to the ranks of Israel, "Why have you come out to draw up for battle? Am I not a Philistine, and are you not servants of Saul? Choose a man for yourselves, and let him come down to me. **9** If he is able to fight with me and kill me, then we will be your servants; but if I prevail against him and kill him, then you shall be our servants and serve us." **10** And the Philistine said, "Today I defy the ranks of Israel! Give me a man, that we may fight together." **11** When Saul and all Israel heard these words of the Philistine, they were dismayed and greatly afraid.
>
> **12** Now David was the son of an Ephrathite of Bethlehem in Judah, named Jesse, who had eight sons. . . . **14** David was the youngest . . . **20** David rose early in the morning, left the sheep with a keeper, took the provisions, and went . . . to the encampment . . . **40** Then he took his staff in his hand, and chose five smooth stones

---

17. See Charlesworth, "The Concept of the Messiah," 188–218; Charlesworth, "From Jewish Messianology to Christian Christology," 225–64; Charlesworth, et al., eds, *The Messiah*; Charlesworth, et al., eds, *Qumran-Messianism*.

from the wadi, and put them in his shepherd's bag, in the pouch; his sling was in his hand, and he drew near to the Philistine.

41 The Philistine came on and drew near to David, with his shield-bearer in front of him. **42** When the Philistine looked and saw David, he disdained him, for he was only a youth, ruddy and handsome in appearance. **43** The Philistine said to David, "Am I a dog, that you come to me with sticks?" And the Philistine cursed David by his gods. **44** The Philistine said to David, "Come to me, and I will give your flesh to the birds of the air and to the wild animals of the field."

45 But David said to the Philistine, "You come to me with sword and spear and javelin; but I come to you in the name of the LORD of hosts, the God of the armies of Israel, whom you have defied. **46** This very day the LORD will deliver you into my hand, and I will strike you down and cut off your head; and I will give the dead bodies of the Philistine army this very day to the birds of the air and to the wild animals of the earth, so that all the earth may know that there is a God in Israel, **47** and that all this assembly may know that the LORD does not save by sword and spear; for the battle is the LORD's and he will give you into our hand."

48 When the Philistine drew nearer to meet David, David ran quickly toward the battle line to meet the Philistine. **49** David put his hand in his bag, took out a stone, slung it, and struck the Philistine on his forehead; the stone sank into his forehead, and he fell face down on the ground. **50** So David prevailed over the Philistine with a sling and a stone, striking down the Philistine and killing him; there was no sword in David's hand. **51** Then David ran and stood over the Philistine; he grasped his sword, drew it out of its sheath, and killed him; then he cut off his head with it.

When the Philistines saw that their champion was dead, they fled. **52** The troops of Israel and Judah rose up with a shout and pursued the Philistines as far as Gath and the gates of Ekron, so that the wounded Philistines fell on the way from Shaaraim as far as Gath and Ekron. **53** The Israelites came back from chasing the Philistines, and they plundered their camp. 54 David took the head of the Philistine and brought it to Jerusalem; but he put his armor in his tent. [NRSV]

Psalm 151 B helps us imagine how Jews celebrated stories of the incredible David. For them, and many millions later, the story was retold how little David dispatched the mighty Goliath. Long before the first century CE, Jews enjoyed retelling such memorable tales around fires, in homes, and in the Temple. Their continuing stress was not so much on David. The focus was on David who proved the awesome unconquerable power of the God of Israel, who was and continues to be present for his faithful ones. What is certain, and centrally important for us in this monograph, is the fact that Jews imagined David was the author of Psalms 151 A and 151 B; many early Jews assumed the passages were, as they claimed, composed by David. It is easy to imagine why Psalm 151 was included in the Greek and Syriac Psalter.[18]

Psalm 152

Psalm 152 is extant only in Syriac. The original language of this psalm seems to be Hebrew. In verse 1 the noun for God is ܐܠܗ which is parallel to the Hebrew word for God, אל; it is not the Syriac name for God, ܐܠܗܐ (cf. 151:3). In verse 6 ܐܕܘܢܝ looks like a (probably confused) transliteration of the Hebrew word for "Lord," אדני, whereas the Syriac name for "Lord" is ܡܪܝܐ (cf. vs. 4). Comparisons of Psalm 152 with Psalms 151, 154, and 155, which are extant in Hebrew and were composed in Hebrew, demonstrate the poor poetic character of this psalm. It seems derivative, uninspired, and a mimic of biblical poetry. If the psalm was composed in Hebrew, the translator probably missed some of the original beauty of the psalm.

---

18. The Non-Masoretic Psalms are not in Samuel Lee's *Vetus Testamentum Syriace* because it is based on the Hebrew canon (*Eos tantum libros sistens qui in canone hebraico habentur*), but see Baars, *The Old Testament in Syriac according to the Peshiṭta Version*.

It is impossible to date Psalm 152. The general tone indicates that the work is Jewish and pre-rabbinic. Associations with Psalms 151, 154, and 155 indicate that it was probably composed by a Palestinian Jew during the Hellenistic period.

Psalm 152 (5ApocSyrPs 4)

Translated from the Syriac

Composed by David after Fighting against the Lion and the Wolf Which Took Sheep from His Flocks.[19]

1 O God,[20] O God, come to my help.
Assist me and save me;
And deliver me[21] from the killers.

2 By the mouth of the lion, shall I descend to Sheol?[22]
Or shall the wolf maim[23] me?[24]

---

19. The title is from MS A; the base text of my translation. The above translation differs from Sanders's idiomatic rendering (*The Dead Sea Psalms Scroll*, 142), because I have attempted to be literal, have occasionally used different manuscripts, and have translated cognate words in these Hebrew and Syriac texts consistently (often missing a beautiful phrase in English).

20. The line is beautiful in Syriac: ܐܠܗܐ ܐܠܗܐ ܬܐ ܠܥܘܕܪܢܝ. The choice of the Hebrew loanword, ܐܠܗܐ (God), seems deliberate to bring out the assonance with ܥܘܕܪܢܝ (to my help). I also contend that this paronomasia is further evidence of a Hebrew original.

21. Or "my soul."

22. See the last verse and "and the gaping abyss."

23. The usual meanings of this verb in Syriac are "to confound," "confuse," and in the *palpel* "to mar," "spoil." Jastrow (*Dictionary*, 172) cites an example in which the verb denotes an action that accelerates death. This meaning is apposite here because of the previous verse, the synonymous parallel, and verse 3c. Perhaps the full verse is shaped by the language of Ps 69:16 and the verb was originally בלע. Its etymology is not clear (see *TWQ* 1:458) and was often mispronounced. The wolf can be imagined by the poet to have swallowed a person, and that verb is linked with Sheol.

24. "Me" is written ܠܝ which is a Hebraism and denotes the *nota accusativi*, with a prefixed redundant ܠ, the Syriac note of the accusative. This observation plus ܐܠܗ for "God" may indicate that this psalm was translated

3 Is it not sufficient for them to ambush my father's flocks;[25]
And to tear a sheep from his sheepfold?
They are even devising to slay me.[26]

4 Spare, O Lord, your elect one,[27]
And deliver your holy one from destruction,
So that he may continue praising you[28] in all his times,
And may praise your magnificent name.[29]

5 When you have saved him from the hands of the vicious wolf[30]
    (and) lion,[31]
And when you have rescued my prey[32] from the mouths of[33]
    beasts.

6 Swiftly, O Adonai,[34] send from your presence a redeemer;[35]
And lift me up from the gaping abyss which is seeking
To enclose me in its depths.

The poetry of Psalm 152, a psalm of individual lament, has a chiasm.[36] The first verse is repeated in v. 4, and "lion" with "wolf" is

---

from Hebrew.

    25. Lit. "to them that they lay in ambush for the flocks of my father."
    26. Or "my soul."
    27. Most Syriac MSS omit "your elect one."
    28. Lit. "continue in your praises."
    29. The poetry flows into the next verse.
    30. Here I leave Manuscript A and follow all other Syriac manuscripts that have "and of the vicious wolf."
    31. The redundancy is unattractive in Manuscript A; all other Syriac manuscripts replace "death" with "lion."
    32. MS A "captivity;" the noun seems ill chosen in MS A. I follow other Syriac manuscripts.
    33. Most Syriac MSS: "hands of."
    34. The Hebrew *Adonai* is employed; by error MS A reads "his Lord."
    35. Or "the Redeemer."
    36. On the linguistic and poetic form called "chiasm," see Welch, ed., *Chiasmus in Antiquity*.

repeated as "wolf" and "lion." The poetry scans into three, two, three, four, two, and three *stichoi* (lines). Again, the poetry is a form of synonymous parallelism. Step parallelism is present in v. 1—that is, the thought moves progressively from "help" to "assist" and finally to "save" and "deliver." In vv. 2–4, "lion" is parallel to "wolf," "flocks" to "sheep," and "your elect one" to "your holy one."

Attribution to David of Psalm 152

In the title, Palm 152 is attributed to David. Many early Jews and Christians obviously assumed David composed it. The author is certainly influenced by the story of David found in 1 Samuel 17:

> **33** Saul said to David, "You are not able to go against this Philistine to fight with him; for you are just a boy, and he has been a warrior from his youth." **34** But David said to Saul, "Your servant used to keep sheep for his father; and whenever a lion or a bear came, and took a lamb from the flock, **35** I went after it and struck it down, rescuing the lamb from its mouth; and if it turned against me, I would catch it by the jaw, strike it down, and kill it. **36** Your servant has killed both lions and bears; and this uncircumcised Philistine shall be like one of them, since he has defied the armies of the living God." **37** David said, "The LORD, who saved me from the paw of the lion and from the paw of the bear, will save me from the hand of this Philistine." [1 Sam 17:33–36; NRSV]

The "lion" appears in 1 Samuel and Psalm 152 but "the bear" of the Hebrew Scripture becomes "wolf." For many early Jews and Christians, this psalm, attributed to David, belonged in the Davidic Psalter. Thus, Psalm 152 was placed in the Syriac Psalter.

Psalm 153

Psalm 153 is extant only in Syriac. The original language cannot be ascertained, but it may be Hebrew. It is conceivable that this psalm was composed in Jerusalem and perhaps in the courts of the Temple. It may antedate the first century CE.

Psalm 153 (5ApocSyrPs 5)

Translated from the Syriac

*Composed by David after Receiving God's Grace
When He Delivered Him from
the Lion and Wolf and Those Two He Killed by His Hands*

1 Praise the LORD, all you nations;
   Glorify him and bless his name;

2 For he delivered the life[37] of his elect one from the hands of death.
   And he redeemed his holy one from destruction.

3 And he saved me[38] from the snares of Sheol;
   And brought me[39] forth from the abyss that is inscrutable.

4 Because before my salvation could proceed from before him,[40]
   I almost became two parts by[41] two beasts.

5 However, he sent his angel and closed from me the gaping mouths;[42]
   And redeemed my life from destruction.

6 I myself[43] shall praise him and exalt him because of all his graces,

---

37. Or "soul."
38. Notice the well-known shift from the third- to the first-person speech.
39. Or "my soul."
40. This is a common Hebrew expression, but Syriac is a Semitic language, and the form could be in an original Syriac composition.
41. The Syriac is inelegant. The adverb "almost" is in the wrong place.
42. Has the author or translator confused the story of David with the story of Daniel in the lions' den?
43. Lit. "my soul."

Which he has provided me and is providing[44] for me.

Psalm 153 shares terms and phrases with Psalm 152; note these: "elect one," "holy one from destruction," "the abyss." The psalms are not identical, but the author of Psalm 153 probably knew Psalm 152 (or *vice versa*).

Psalm 153 is a hymn of thanksgiving and chiastic, with v. 1 repeated by v. 6 and v. 2 by v. 5. It is constructed with six *bicola*, and the style is again synonymous *parallelismus membrorum*—that is, the second line echoes the memory obtained from the first line. Notably, "praise" is synonymous with "glorify" and "bless," "delivered" with "redeemed," "his elect one" with "his holy one," "saved" with "brought forth," and "Sheol" with "the abyss." By observing these parallels, scholars learn the meaning of some opaque terms.

Attribution to David of Psalm 153

David is mentioned only in the inscription. In light of Psalm 152, in which "your elect one" and "your holy one" are sobriquets for David, many Jews, familiar with the Psalter, would identify "his elect one" and "his holy one" with David so that all the nations will glorify the LORD. Thus, the "two beasts" with "gaping mouths" would be the lion and the wolf who threatened David, according to Psalm 152. An organic relation exists between these Non-Masoretic Psalms;[45] thus, Psalm 152 would be earlier than Psalm 153.

Psalm 153 offers an explanation to a difference between the Hebrew and Syriac of Psalm 151 A. In the Hebrew of Psalm 151 A, we are told that God "sent his prophet" to David "to anoint me." In the Syriac of Psalm 151 A, however, we read that God "sent his angel . . . and anointed me with the ointment of his anointing." The latter thought shapes Psalm 153 (extant only in Syriac) so that God "sent his angel" to redeem the speaker (David) from the two beasts "and delivered my life from destruction." Those who note that the

---

44. Or "will provide"; the verb is an active participle.

45. See my comments in Charlesworth and Sanders, "More Psalms of David," 609.

references to angels increase from *1 Enoch* 1–36 (dated to perhaps 300 BCE) to *4QŠirŠabb, Pseudo-Philo, Testament of Job, 2 Enoch, 3 Baruch, Testament of Abraham*, and the *Apocalypse of Abraham* will conclude rightly that Psalm 151 A in Syriac and Psalm 153 in Syriac postdate the first century CE. We should imagine that a redactor in Syriac made changes to Hebrew texts.

Psalm 154

The original language of Psalm 154 is Hebrew, and it is preserved in 11QPs^a (11Q5). Because the psalm is preserved in this first-century-BCE manuscript, it must date from the early first or (better) the second century BCE.[46] There is no reason to doubt that it was composed somewhere in Palestine, perhaps in the early stages of the Essene sect.

Among Psalms 151–155, Psalm 154 is most closely aligned with the thoughts produced during the early years of the Essenes who eventually resided at Qumran.[47] The "many ones" (or "Many") of 154:1 (only in Syriac; the Hebrew is lost) may be parallel to "the Many," a technical term (רַבִּים) that defines the initiated member of the Qumran Community (see 1QS 6.8–7.25). The "many" probably no longer has a generic denotation, as it does in 155:10 and Isa 53:11. The Hebrew of 154:4, which has been translated "Join an assembly," certainly meant at Qumran "join the *Yaḥad* (יחד)." As is universally recognized, the latter is a technical term at Qumran for the Community of oneness in covenant with God (eg. 1QH 11.10–14; 3.19–23).[48] Other nouns that are technical terms at Qumran,

---

46. Most of the Non-Masoretic Psalms in 11QPs^a are from the second century BCE. See Cross, "The History of the Biblical Text," 177–95, esp. 182; Hurvitz, "Observations on the Language," 225–32; Polzin, "Notes on the Dating," 468–76; and Skehan, *Qumrân*, 168.

47. See Charlesworth and Sanders, "More Psalms of David," 610 n. 7 and the references to Dupont-Sommer, Philonenko, and Delcor, all of whom were convinced Psalm 154 was composed within the Qumran Community.

48. See especially Wernberg-Møller, "The Nature of the YAHAD according to the Manual of Discipline," 56–81; and Pouilly, *La Règle de la Communauté de Qumrân*, 102–7.

but not necessarily ideas peculiar to the Dead Sea Scrolls, are "the innocent ones" in 154:3, 18 (cf. 1QS 4.22) and "the poor ones" in 154:18 (cf. 1QH 2.43, 5.13–14). Concepts cherished at Qumran are the ideas expressed in 154:10–11 (that the Most High accepts praise as equal to sacrifices) and in 154:13–14 (that the righteous share in common meals and constantly study the Torah or Law).[49] My judgment, finally, is that while there is nothing peculiarly Qumranic about Psalm 154, it may antedate the exodus of the Jews to Qumran and represent some of the earliest Essenes' concepts.[50] In contrast to my earlier translations in *OTP* 2 and PTSDSS 4A, I have chosen to highlight a translation that aligns Psalm 154 with the early Essenes of the late second century BCE.

Psalm 154 (11QPsa 154)

Translated from the Hebrew (and Syriac in vv. 1–2, 18–20)

1 In a great voice glorify[51] God;
In the congregation of the Many[52] proclaim his glory.

2 And in the multitude of the upright ones glorify his excellence;
And with the faithful ones narrate his gloriousness.

---

49. Skehan states that "it is interesting that this, Ps 154, is a reflex of the Essene religious assemblies and communal meals." See Skehan *Qumrân*, 169.

50. Sanders shows that the psalm portrays "three distinct groups": the righteous, those addressed by them, and the wicked. I agree with Sanders that this psalm is "proto-Essenian, or Hasidic." See Sanders, *The Psalms Scroll of Qumran Cave 11*, 69–70. In my estimation, the psalm dates from the earliest years of the Essene sect.

51. In Pss 151–153 שבח is translated as "praise"; here in Syriac it denotes "glory." Uppermost in the poet's mind is the concept of glorifying (or praising) God's glory. The root שבע or its cognates appear in vv. 1 (*bis*), 3, 4, 7, 10, and 17. The cognate masculine noun is translated "glory"; the feminine noun with the same meaning, תשבוחתא (using Hebrew script) in 154:2 is distinguished as "gloriousness."

52. "The congregation of the Many" is a technical term in the Dead Sea Scrolls as we know from 1QS, but it no longer retained this meaning in the latter Syriac-speaking churches.

Has Psalm 156 Been Found?

3   [Associate][53] yourselves[54] with the good ones;
    And with the Perfect Ones[55] glorify the Most High.

4   Form a Community[56] to announce his salvation.
    And do not be lax to announce his power,
    And his gloriousness[57] to all simple ones.

5   For to announce the glory[58] of the LORD,
    Wisdom has been given.

6   And to recount his many deeds,
    She was made known to humanity:

7   To announce to simple ones his power,
    To explain to those lacking understanding his greatness,[59]

8   Those far from her (Wisdom's) openings,[60]
    Those banished from her entrances.

---

53. The Hebrew of 154:1–43a is lost; the verb "associate" is restored from the Syriac. The translation is an attempt to render the Syriac and Hebrew versions so that the cognate (and corresponding) words within each are easily recognized.

54. Or "your souls."

55. The Qumran Essenes called themselves "the Perfect Ones." See esp. 1QS 2.2; 3.2, 9; 4.22; 6.17; 8.1; 9. 10, 18, 20, 21; 9.2, 5 6, 8, 9, 19.

56. The Hebrew is יחד; that is a technical term at Qumran, which meant the Community of oneness in covenant with God. See esp. 1QS cols. 1, 2, 3, 5, 6, 7, 8, 9, 10 and 1QH esp. cols. 6. 11, 12, 13, 14, 16, 18, 19.

57. The Hebrew noun for "gloriousness" (154:4, 9) is cognate with "to glorify" in 154:3b, 10a, 17a, and with "glory" in 154:5a. The theme of the psalm is clearly to glorify God's glory, as is demonstrated by the first two verses, preserved only in Syriac: "to glorify God ... proclaim his glory ... glorify his excellence ... narrate his gloriousness." Wisdom (v. 5) was given to accomplish this task.

58. Or "honor."

59. Sanders has: "and to explain to senseless folk his greatness ..." (*The Dead Sea Psalms Scroll*, 105).

60. Or "doorways," "openings," or "utterances." The double entendre is

9 Because the Most High is the Lord of Jacob,
And his gloriousness (is) over all his deeds.

10 And a person who glorifies the Most High,
He accepts as one who brings a meal offering,

11 As one who offers he-goats and baby bulls;
As one who anoints the altar with many burnt offerings;
As sweet-smelling fragrance from the hand of the righteous ones.

12 From the openings[61] of the righteous ones is heard her (Wisdom's) voice;
And from the congregation of the pious ones her song.

13 When they eat with satiety she is cited;
And when they drink in fellowship together.

14 Their meditation is on the Torah of the Most High;
Their words[62] are to announce his power.

15 How far from the wicked ones (is) her word;[63]
From all the haughty ones to know her.

16 Behold, the eyes of the Lord
Will be upon the good ones with compassion;

---

found only in Hebrew. Wisdom's "openings" are associated with her "utterances." The paronomasia increases the evidence of Hebrew being the language of composition.

61. Or "utterances." The play on words is possible in Hebrew, but not in Syriac. Thus, the Hebrew is superior and the original language (otherwise we would need to conclude that the Syriac translator was superior to the Hebrew scribe, but this conclusion is unlikely, as these comments show).

62. Or "citings"; see 154:13a

63. Or "citing."

17 And upon those who glorify him will he increase his mercy;
From an evil time will he deliver them.[64]

18 [Blessed be] the LORD who saves the Poor Ones from the hand of strangers.
And redeems the innocent ones from the hand of the evil ones,

19 Who raises the horn from Jacob,
And the judge of the nations from Israel.

20 So that he may prolong his sojourn in Zion.
And may cause adornment forever in Jerusalem.

Notice the refined poetry of Psalm 154. Again, it mirrors the Davidic Psalter and displays in twenty verses a series of *bicola* with vv. 4 and 11 having three lines. The psalm is another example of synonymous *parallelismus membrorum*.

Most prominent is a set of terms that have similar meanings and define two groups of Jews. The early Essenes are most likely designated as "the upright ones," "the faithful ones," "the good ones," "the Perfect Ones," "the righteous ones," "the pious ones," "those who glorify him," and "the Poor Ones." Probably reflecting the enemies of the Essenes, the Hasmoneans in charge of the Temple cult, are "all simple ones," "those lacking understanding," "the wicked ones," "the haughty ones," "strangers," and "the evil ones." As is clear from the *Rule of the Community* and the *Thanksgiving Hymns*, Essene theology is also found in the rejection of the Temple cult and the emphasis on praise as the proper worship for God: "And a person who glorifies the Most High" is one whom the deity accepts "as one who brings a meal offering," "he-goats," "baby bulls," and "as one who anoints the altar with many burnt offerings" (154:10–11 in Hebrew). Perhaps Psalm 154 was composed in the early Essene sect.

---

64. Or "their soul."

INTRODUCTIONS AND TRANSLATIONS OF PSALMS 151–155

Attribution of Psalm 154.

Psalm 154 celebrates Wisdom, and she seems personified; she was given to humanity "to announce the glory of the LORD," as well as to recount the LORD's "many deeds" and "power." There is no reason to assume or conclude that Psalm 154 was composed by or imagined as a composition by David. Rather than a reminiscence of David's life, the psalm is an exhortation to praise God so he will reside permanently in Zion, Jerusalem. In the Syriac, Psalm 154 is attributed to Hezekiah: "The Prayer of Hezekiah When the Assyrians Were Surrounding Him and He Was Asking God's Deliverance from Them So That the People Might Receive Permission from Cyrus to Return to Their Land. And They Asked God to Fulfill Their Expectation."[65] The non-Davidic traditions define a psalm globally saluted as "Psalm 154." That insight will be pertinent when we evaluate the Davidic dimensions of Psalm 156.

Psalm 155

Psalm 155 was composed in Hebrew. A broken alphabetic acrostic in Hebrew flows from at least lines 8 to 12 of the Hebrew manuscript (11Q5) or vv. 9–13 (ט ח ז ו ה). Lines 3–7, according to 11Q5, or verses 1–8, preserve a staccato plea for deliverance in 2/2 meter.

As with Psalm 154, the Syriac appears to derive directly from the Hebrew.[66] The psalm was composed neither in the early Essene sect nor at Qumran. It antedates Qumran and is biblical. It is defined by exhortations to the LORD. It is similar in style to Psalm 22, especially the opening three verses. Psalm 22 is called "A Psalm of David" and begins with these words so familiar to all who read the Psalter:

1 My God, my God, why have you forsaken me?

---

65. The title is from MS A, but it is very late and has little relation to the content of the psalm.

66. See Strugnell ("Notes on the Text," 275–76) and the notes to the translation.

Why are you so far from helping me, from the words of my
groaning?

2 O my God, I cry by day, but you do not answer;
And by night, but find no rest.
3 Yet you are holy,
Enthroned on the praises of Israel. [NRSV]

Since it is extant in 11QPs[a] (11Q5), it must antedate the first century BCE and is probably much earlier. The Syriac translator is gifted;[67] he cannot be identified with the translator of Psalms 152 and 153. Like most of the canonical (or Masoretic) psalms,[68] this psalm is generic in thought and tone; hence it is impossible to ascertain more precisely the author, date, or provenience.

Psalm 155 (11QPs[a] 155)

Translated from the Hebrew (and Syriac in vv. 18b–21)

1 O LORD, I cry unto you,
Be attentive to me.

2 I spread forth my palms,
Toward your holy dwelling.

3 Incline your ear;
And give me my request.

4 And my petition
Do not hold back from me.

---

67. See the notes to both translations.
68. In Hebrew it is constructed in acrostics; see Skehan, "A Broken Acrostic and Psalm 9," 1–5; Auffret, "Structure littéraire et interpretation du Psaume 155," 323–56; and Magne, "Le Psaume 154," 95–102; and Magne, "Le Psaume 155," 103–11.

Introductions and Translations of Psalms 151–155

5 Build me[69] up;
And do not cast me down.

6 And do no abandon (me)
Before the wicked ones.

7 The rewards of evil,
May the Judge of Truth remove from me.

8 O Lord, do not condemn me according to my sins;
For no one living is righteous before you.

9 O Lord, instruct me in your Torah;
And teach me your statutes;[70]

10 So[71] many may hear of your deeds,
And nations may honor your magnificence.[72]

11 Remember me and do not forget me;
And do not allow me to enter that which is too difficult for me.[73]

12 The sins of my youth cast far from me;
And my transgressions do not remember against me.

13 O Lord, purify me from the evil plague;
And do not let it again turn back to me.

---

69. Or "my soul."

70. The expression "your statutes" is cognate with "do not condemn me" in 155:8.

71. Lit. "and."

72. Or "glory," "honor."

73. This is probably the original meaning of "the Lord's Prayer," but the Greek translator missed the permissive *hiphil* or *aphel*.

14 Dry up its roots from me;
   And do not let its le[av]es[74] bloom in me.

15 Magnificent are you, O Lord;
   Hence complete my request from before you.

16 To whom may I cry and he would give to me?
   And human beings, what can [their] pow[er] add?[75]

17 Befo[r]e you, O Lord, is my trust.
   I cried, "O Lord," and he answered me;
   [And he healed][76] my broken heart.

18 I slumbered [and I s]lept;[77]
   I dreamed, nevertheless I was aroused.

19 And you supported me, O Lord.
   And I shall render (thanks) because the Lord delivered me.

20 Now I shall behold their shame;
   I trusted in you and shall not be ashamed.
   Give honor (to the Lord) forever and ever.

21 Save Israel, your elect one;
   And those of the house of Jacob, your chosen one.

Notice the refined poetry of Psalm 155; it preserves a partial alphabetic acrostic. In Hebrew, these verses are crafted as a series of *bicola*, with v. 17 having three lines (and line 20 in Syriac has three lines). Psalm 155 is another example of synonymous *parallelismus membrorum*. Hence, we learn that "your Torah" is parallel to "your

---

74. Restored in Hebrew but extant in Syriac.
75. Syriac: "And human beings, what can their strength add (for me)?"
76. Restored to the Hebrew; extant in Syriac.
77. Restored to the Hebrew; extant in Syriac.

statutes," and "your deeds" reveal "your magnificence." Reminiscent of the Lord's Prayer is verse 11b: "and do not allow me to enter that which is too difficult for me."

Attribution of Psalm 155

If the Hebrew manuscript from Cave IV had a title, it is now lost. A Syriac scribe attributes the psalm to Hezekiah: "*The Prayer of Hezekiah When the Assyrians Surrounded Him and He Asked God's Deliverance from Them.* This title is from Syriac MS A and is late; it should not inform us of the original attribution. David composed Psalms 151–155 according to the end of the Psalter in MS A of the twelfth century CE:[78] "So ends, by the assistance of our LORD, the copying of the Psalms of the blessed David, the prophet and king, with the five psalms that are not among the Greek or Hebrew numbering. However, as they are said (and) preserved in Syriac so we have copied them for him who desires (a copy)."

Conclusion

We have translated and examined the poetry and attribution of Psalms 151–155. These are five psalms, related to the Psalter in numerous ways, and some are clearly attributed to David, Israel's second and greatest king. Now we may turn to a psalm found in the famous Cairo Genizah which preserves some very ancient Jewish documents. While the manuscript dates from the Middle Ages, it preserves a psalm that is ancient and belongs within Early Judaism—that is, the psalm dates certainly from 300 BCE to 200 CE. As I will disclose, all experts who have examined it now recognize the antiquity of what may be MS RNL Antonin 798.

---

78. MS A was in the Library of the Chaldean Patriarchate in Baghdad. It was formerly in Mosul. It was known as MS 1113 [for the Non-Masoretic Psalms, see fols. 118b–20b]. The wars in Baghdad and Mosul could have destroyed this valuable manuscript.

Has Psalm 156 Been Found?

Is this psalm, that is virtually unknown to biblical scholars, linked to the Davidic Psalter? Using the methodology already employed, and accepted universally by Jews and Christians, I will seek to ascertain if it is "Psalm 156." Thus, we turn to the next chapter in which we present the text and translation of MS RNL Antonin 798.

2

Translation of MS RNL Antonin 798

Numerous medieval manuscripts were found in the Cairo Genizah. One is now preserved in the Antonin Collection at the National Library in Saint Petersburgh and is known as "MS RNL Antonin 798." As intimated in the previous chapter, this psalm may be ancient. Was it composed in the Temple before 100 BCE?

This manuscript is difficult to translate from Hebrew to English.[1] Perhaps one reason is that much was lost when it was transcribed, numerous times, from about 100 BCE to the eighth or tenth century CE. As one might then expect, the Hebrew generally lacks the refinement found intermittently in the *Thanksgiving Hymns*, some of which were composed at Qumran under the influence of the Righteous Teacher. The Qumranites wrote in elegant Hebrew; especially in the early decades of the Community since many Qumranites were Aaronite priests or Levites. I have arranged the text according to early Jewish poetry with reflections on the transmission of the medieval manuscript, and prepared an idiomatic translation for general readers.[2]

---

1. For images and a transcription of the manuscript, see Appendix 2.

2. For a more literal translation and critical philological notes, see my text and translation (assisted by Lea Berkuz) in the PTSDSSP 9A, in press.

Has Psalm 156 Been Found?

Translation

Col. 1

God the Cosmic Judge and Creator[3]

1 (‏ג‎)[4] Revealed before you (O God, are)[5] the righteous and the wicked.[6]
And you seek[7] not for them human witnesses.[8]

2 (‏ד‎) (You are) the Judge[9] of generations and the Ruler[10] in righteousness.
You make known the ways of all life.[11]

3 (‏ח‎)[12] You delight (with those) in righteousness but despise (those) in iniquity.
And the boastful ones will never stand in the presence of your glory.

---

3. The titles are provided by Charlesworth, the translator.

4. An acrostic (meaning that the psalm has been crafted with skill so that each successive verse begins with the next letter in the Hebrew alphabet) begins here; the beginning is probably lost, though it might be misplaced at the end.

5. Ancient Hebrew, as in MS RNL Antonin 798, is cryptic; hence, often the translator must add verbs and *nomen regens* in parentheses.

6. See Ezek 21:8–9 and Ps 11:5; cf. 1QH[a] 12.39 and CD Manuscript B 2.20–21. Notice the two groups but the absence of the *termini technici* of the dualism in 1QS 3.13–4.26.

7. The imperfects denote completed action in the present.

8. Lit. "witnesses of Adam."

9. God as Judge helps define MS RNL Antonin 798.

10. Lit. "one ruling."

11. Or "all living beings." This expression appears only at Qumran, among early Jewish texts; see 1QH[a] 7.35.

12. The next letter should be a *he* and not a *ḥet*; why did this occur? Did he pronounce these letters similarly? Was the script Hasmonean, in which the two consonants are often indistinguishable?

4 (ו) And you divided the world between darkness and light,[13]
 And between impurity and purity and between falsehood and righteousness.[14]

God's Purified and Renewed Nation[15]

5 (ז) You cast off from your people all the sons of foreigners;
 And you purified your flock from impure beasts.[16]

6 (ח) Your mighty wisdom you gave to your servant,[17]
 That he might understand in all things[18] the desires of your will.[19]

7 (ט) You (O God) planted righteous ones in the land of truth.[20]
 And justice you multiplied throughout the world.[21]

---

13. See Genesis 1; note the foreshadowing of Qumran's dualism in many pre-Qumranic documents, notably Isa 11:4; Pss 9:9, 72:2, 96:13, and 98:9.

14. This line sounds very similar to 1QS, notably its dualism in 3.13—4.26.

15. The perfects may be examples of *perfectum futurum*, a verbal form in which the past is used to describe the certainty of future events. The following lines are not eschatological. They celebrate the victories and harmony of the early Hasmoneans.

16. An emphasis found in Ezra and Nehemiah.

17. The following lines clarify that David is "your servant." See 1.15 and col. 2.

18. Lit. "in all of them."

19. See 3.1, 4, and CD 3.15, "the desires of his will." Also see Eph 1:5.

20. See Isaiah 5 and esp. 1QH^a 16; *PssSol* 14:2; and *OdesSol* 11:18–19. The "righteous ones" are "planted." Here "the land of truth" is the Holy Land, not Paradise. Similar concepts appear in *1 En* 93; note 4QEn^g 1.4 in which the elect ones are "from the eternal plant of righteousness" (or "truth") and are "witnesses to righteousness."

21. Not "eternity" because of parallelism with "the land." Lit. "in all the worlds."

Has Psalm 156 Been Found?

8 (ו) All the worshipers of[22] your name[23] will learn a (new) chant,[24]
Those who will believe[25] in the words of your servant.[26]

9 (ב) In the presence of all (those in) the land, they will multiply their righteousness,
And assure[27] their prosperity (with those)[28] they love in their heart.

10 (ד)[29] You established their way[30] towards your commandments.
And you strengthened[31] their power through all your wondrous works.

11 (ל) For ever and ever they will worship[32] your name.
And for eternity to eternities they will exalt your name.[33]

---

22. Lit. "work" or "serve." A frequent expression in the Hebrew Bible; see esp. Ps 100:2. The passage probably refers to the priests and Levites in the Jerusalem Temple.

23. In col. 1, the poet seems to prefer "your name" for the *Tetragrammaton*; see "your name" in 1.8, 11 [*bis*], 26; cf. "his (God's) name" in 1.17, 19. Also see "the name of the Great One," 1.22. In col. 2, the *Tetragrammaton* appears without distinction; see lines 1, 3, 5, 6, 12, 16.

24. Lit. "they will learn a chant (song)." See "a new chant (song)" as in Ps 40:4. Chanting, not singing, defines worship in Judaism.

25. Or "trust."

26. See line 15: "David your servant." David, God's servant, seems intended. From such Jewish concepts the Fourth Evangelist crafted his Gospel.

27. Lit. "doers of their prosperity."

28. The Hebrew makes sense only in idiomatic English.

29. Perhaps the scribe's distinction between medial and final forms means that in Early Judaism some Jews saw final forms as distinct individual consonants. Sometimes the *waw* in Hasmonean script appears a final form.

30. At Qumran "the Way" becomes a *terminus technicus*. This poem or hymn antedates Qumran.

31. This is a Hebrew form that postdates 70 CE; see *Bereshith Rabba* 54. See *Even-Shoshan Dictionary*, 3:1003. Is this word a product of the medieval copiers?

32. Lit. "workers of."

33. Beginning with the next bicola, the author seems to accept final forms

12 (מ) Who can match your works and who can match your deeds.[34] And who can resemble you[35] concerning the grandeur[36] of all your works?[37]

God's Forgiveness

13 (ס) You pardoned[38] and you forgave all our sins. And you atoned with love for all our transgressions.[39]

14 (נ) You prophesied through your spirit[40] by the mouth of your servant;[41]

---

as a separate orthography. Thus, *mem* medial and final are two consonants.

34. Lit. "Who like your works and who like your deeds." See "doers" in a note in line 9.

35. See Exod 15:11.

36. Lit. "greatness," or "multitude."

37. See the *Self-Glorification Hymn*, in which we hear about "who can resemble me." The author creates a polemic against all foreign gods, as in the Davidic Psalter. Here probably the author has in mind Zeus or Jupiter, the supreme god of the Greeks and Romans; cf. Antiochus Epiphanes's attempt to establish a temple to Zeus in the Jerusalem Temple.

38. מחל is not a biblical verb. It appears in the Mishnah; see *Even-Shoshan Dictionary*, 3:1296. Is this word an example of rabbinic Hebrew at Qumran, as in some Qumran Scrolls, or the evidence of transmission to maybe the tenth century?

39. Notice the emphasis on "love" in this text; also see 1.26; 2.6, 23.

40. Notice the author does not refer to "the Holy Spirit." This text probably antedates Qumran because, as most scholars note, "the Holy Spirit" is a creation of the Essenes or Qumranites.

41. David is "your servant," a theme that defines 1 Chronicles and many other texts. Notably, see the psalm attributed to David in 1 Chr 16:13 and 17:4, 7, 24, 25 [*bis*], 26, 27. Also see 2 Sam 7:19–29; Pss 89:2, 4, 21.

For you have brought near[42] the Endtime;[43] and you will delay (it) no more.[44]

Honoring David

15 (ק) You made a pledge ahead[45] to David your servant;[46]
And you anointed[47] with compassion the Shoot of Jesse.[48]

16 (ס) You sustained his arm[49] through your holiness,[50]
For he established your praise unto the ends of the earth.[51]

---

42. The text has "I approach"; the orthography is clear, and the scribe of the manuscript distinguishes between the *waw* and the *yod*. Ignore the *yod*; it either is an error by the author or was incorrectly added in transmission. The first-person discourse does not appear in col. 1 of this document. The second-person singular perfect dominates in the entire text; note the contiguous lines: 10 (*bis*), 13 (three times), 14 (plus this error), 15, 16, and 17.

43. Frequently in Jewish compositions before 70 CE, we hear about the Endtime no longer being delayed.

44. See Isa 60:22, Sir 36:10, and 1QpHab 7.

45. See Isa 40:21, "from the beginning," but that refers to creation and Genesis. See esp. 1 Chr 16:7, according to which David "first" delivered a thanksgiving psalm to YHWH. "Ahead" brings out the paronomasia between "David," "head," and "chief." See *OdesSol* 24:1. The link between "chief" and "first" comes out in line 18b.

46. David is explicitly mentioned only here. See the note to 4.25a. In the *Targum Isaiah* is the tradition that "my servant" is "the Messiah" (*TgIsa* 52:13).

47. Note the absence of any clear messianic overtones.

48. This claim seems to antedate Qumran. Neither the Hasmoneans nor the Qumranites were descendants of David, but some affirmed the Davidic Messiah. While this passage is possibly messianic, the *terminus technicus* "Messiah" is not present. See *Amidah* 14 (the old Palestinian Version): "Have compassion, O LORD our God . . . upon the royal seed of David, your justly anointed one."

49. See Jer 48:25 and Ps 10:15. For the expression "the arm of the LORD," see Isa 51:5, 9 and 53:1.

50. A *bet* that designates the dative of means.

51. Not "land." This line is an echo of Isa 52:10: "The LORD has made bare his holy arm in the eyes of all the nations. And all the ends of the earth shall see the salvation of our God." Our author may be thinking about Solomon's

17 (ע) (As) an eternal pillar[52] you set his name.
And he is breaking through the wall[53] and rebuilding the ruins.[54]

18 (פ) (David is) a cornerstone despised which the builders despised;[55]
And you raised (him) to be head[56] above all the nations.[57]

19 (ף) Magnificence[58] and a crown[59] you have allowed him to inherit with rejoicing.
And the splendor of all the Gentiles you are calling his name.[60]

20 (צ) Righteousness and justice you multiplied in his (David's) days.
And peace and blessings[61] forever without number.

---

relation with Ethiopia and the Queen of Sheba in 1 Kings 10.

52. See Gal 2:9. The author highlights David's name as an eternal memorial. See *b. Hagîgâ* 12b in which we are told that the world rests on the unique column called the righteous one.

53. A wall made of stones without mortar. See a similar expression in Isa 5:5 and Ps 80:13[12].

54. Note the participles. See Isa 58:12. The thought is not clear; it may refer to how David and Joab broke into Jerusalem and that ruins could still be seen in and around Jerusalem after numerous wars. The emphasis is upon David, who restores Zion, Jerusalem.

55. Note the inelegant Hebrew. The author has memorized Ps 118:22, "The stone which the builders rejected has become the chief cornerstone."

56. Or "head," "chief."

57. Cf. Ps 118:22.

58. Or "beauty."

59. See 2 Sam 12:30.

60. Note the author's use of different nouns for "nation." See 1.5 עם, "people," in 1.18 אומים, "nations," and in 1.19 גוים, "Gentiles." God's chosen people are עם; the foreign nations are אומים and גוים.

61. "Blessings" is the title of the *Thanksgiving Hymns*; see the announcement of the discovery of the handle sheet of 1QH[a] in PTSDSSP 5A.

Has Psalm 156 Been Found?

Future Rejoicing as God Supports David

21 (צ) All the elect ones of righteousness shout for joy before you,
   For they will be happy in the pleasant[62] land.[63]

22 (ק) You made holy through his (David's) mouth the name of the Great One (O God).[64]
   And the chants of your strength[65] he recounts[66] each day.

23 (ר) Above[67] all the angels you made his greatness.[68]
   And king of all the nations you placed him for eternity.[69]

24 (ש) You broke before him all the kings of Midian.[70]
   And you drowned in the depths[71] those who hate him.[72]

---

62. Or "delilghtful," "lovely," or "beloved." See Ps 106:24, "the pleasant land," which refers to Moses and the rebellious people who "despised" the Promised Land.

63. The noun ארץ denotes both "earth" and "land" (the Holy Land) in this poem. See 1.7, 16, and 21.

64. See Ezek 36:23.

65. Cf. Ps 59:17, the *Self-Glorification Hymn*, and the New Testament claims for Jesus.

66. The imperfect: "he shall recount."

67. This noun in biblical Hebrew also means "multitude," "abundance."

68. See the *Self-Glorification Hymn* in PTSDSSP 5A. The author attributes to David the claim that he is higher than all the angels. That is an unusual thought in Early Judaism.

69. Cf. Ps 89:28.

70. Cf. Isa 9:3.

71. This is an allusion to God's mighty deliverance of the Hebrews from Egyptian bondage. It is an incredible claim since David lived about three centuries after Moses. The author probably knew that fact, but he is a poet and not a historian.

72. "Him" translates נפשו, "his soul," but that translation might suggest Greek anthropology.

Translation of MS RNL Antonin 798

25 (ת) You supported his right arm[73] over his sword.
And you strengthened his arm over the mighty-warriors of Kedar.[74]

26 (ל)[75] His leg will not stagger[76] for he trusted through your name.[77]
And his power will not stumble for you helped him through love.[78]

A Beatitude

27 (א)[79] Fully joyful[80] is the man[81] who will trust in your Word,[82]
For his face was not shamed[83] for ever and ever.

Col. 2

Beatitudes[84]

1 (ב) In you my being[85] trusts; O favor me and answer me.

---

73. See note in line 16.
74. Kedar denotes an Arabian tribe; see Gen 25:13, Ezek 27:21, Ps 120:5 and esp. Isa 21:16–17 where Isaiah twice refers to the warriors of Kedar.
75. Why is *lamed* inserted here in the acrostic?
76. See Ps 121:3.
77. See Ezek 36:23.
78. See 1.13 and the emphasis on love.
79. Note that the ʾ*aleph* and *bet* of the acrostic are now possibly misplaced. Either the beginning of the acrostic is lost with the beginning of the psalm, or the beginning is placed at the end possibly due to mistakes during the transmission of this psalm from Jerusalem to Qumran, copying at Qumran, and then copying more than once until about the eighth or tenth century CE.
80. Chosen to represent a beatitude since "blessed" is reserved for ברוך.
81. Heb. הגבר.
82. Probably God's word in the Davidic Psalms. Cf. Ps 40:5, "in the Lord." The claim is not convincing that the acrostic begins here.
83. Or "humiliated."
84. See Appendix 1, in which the most important beatitudes in Early Judaism and Christian Origins are listed.
85. Or "soul;" though it is best not to translate as "soul" since it would

Blessed are you, O LORD,[86] (the) God who answers his servant[87] each[88] time he calls.

2 O God of mercy, have mercy upon us.
Blessed is the name of his glorious kingdom[89] for ever and ever.

3 Blessed is the name of his glory[90] for ever and ever.
Blessed is the LORD, the God of Israel,[91] from eternity and (unto) eternity.[92]

4 And all the people said: "Amen."[93]

---

remind some readers of bifurcated Greek anthropology. The Semitic concept of the human is unified as one whole.

86. The *Tetragrammaton* is written full and without distinction in this column: יהוה. The text does not then seem to be a Qumran or early Rabbinic composition. At Qumran the *Tetragrammaton* is avoided or written in palaeo-Hebrew or with *tetrapuncta* (four dots as in 1QS 8.14). In Rabbinics it is abbreviated. Of course, a transcribing scribe, esp. in the Middle Ages, would have probably altered the original way of writing the *Tetragrammaton* if the form was not familiar to him.

87. "Servant" here seems to denote the faithful one who calls on God.

88. Lit. "in each." The Hebrew seems unrefined. Perhaps the *bet* was added in transmission.

89. The author does not inform us if "his" refers to God or to David. Most likely, the author would have answered that the pronoun was intended to denote both (*double entente*).

90. The expression "his glory" refers to God's glory; that is clarified by the synonymous parallelism.

91. The Qumranites blessed "the God of Knowledge."

92. See 3.8–9 and 4.14–15. See esp. the second psalm attributed to David in 1 Chr 29:10, "And David said, 'Blessed are you, O LORD, the God of Israel, our Father, from eternity and unto eternity.'" Note our poet does call the LORD "our Father." See also 2 Sam 7:14 and 1 Chr 17:13, "I shall be to him (David) Father, and he shall be to me son."

93. "Amen" ends the previous thought, but it does not end one psalm and begin another. See 1 Chr 16:36, "And they said, all the people, 'Amen.'" Notice our author understands "people" as a collective for Israel. All the people praise "the God of Israel." The text probably does not represent the remnant ideology of the Essenes or Qumranites.

TRANSLATION OF MS RNL ANTONIN 798

First Vision (Concerning David's Vision of "The Faithful One")[94]

5 In the month of Iyyar[95] on the second (day)[96] in the month,
   I[97] saw in a vision and all his[98] prophecies.
   And I prayed before the LORD and I said:

6 "May your mercy, O LORD our God, be upon the slaughtered sheep,[99]
   Which the shepherds[100] slaughtered and had no compassion upon them.[101]

7 With your mercy bind up the tender bones.[102]
   And with (your)[103] love[104] heal the brokenness of your inheritance.[105]

---

94. Stec, Philonenko, and Marx judged that a new psalm began here.

95. The festival of Shavuot occurs in Iyyar, when the Torah was given. In *Guide for the Perplexed* (3:43), Maimonides states that the counting of the Omer is a time which requires spiritual preparation. The *Zohar* (see 3:97a–b) connects the counting of days for the period of impurity for women (Lev 15:28) and says just as women need to be purified, so did the Israelites need to be purified as they left Egypt to go to Sinai and receive the Torah.

96. Supposedly, Iyyar days 1 and 2 appeared previously in this truncated scroll.

97. The "I" is ambiguous, it could be Judas Maccabeus, another Hasmonean, or an imagined David. The flow of this psalm suggests the "I" is intended to be David.

98. "His" refers to God.

99. See Ps 44:23. For some inexplicable reason, Flusser's translation misses one line of the Hebrew.

100. As in *1 Enoch*, the shepherds represent evil rulers. The noun "sheep" refers to God's people, a thought well known from Psalm 23.

101. See *1 En* 89:19, 90:25; cf. Zech 11:4, 7.

102. See Gen 18:7. These lines do not refer to slaughtered sheep. See Ps 51:10 with LXX (not MT).

103. One would expect the *parallelismus membrorum* to have a "your."

104. See the note to 1.13.

105. See Mic 7:4, נחלתך צאן; the reference is to God's people, the inheritance. Also see Ps 147:3.

8 Because for the good of the world you have allowed me (David)
     to stand before you.[106]
   And for a light (to) the Gentiles you commissioned[107] me with
     your strength.

9 All the nations will recount your glory.[108]
   For they will see your righteousness through the hand of your
     faithful one.[109]

10 Let them gather: The officials and all the kings of the earth,
   The princes[110] of the inhabited-world,[111] the rulers of the human,[112]

11 So they may see the mighty (deeds)[113] of your right hand,
   And to discern the mystery[114] of your holy words.[115]

12 Then all of them[116] will comprehend[117] your might.

---

106. See the parallel thoughts in Isa 42:6, 49:6, and esp. 11Q5 27.2, in which David is "a light like the light of the sun."

107. Lit. "granted." The poet quotes the famous passage about "the light to the Gentiles" found in Isa 49:6 ונתתיך לאור גוים. See also Isa 42:6 and *LAB* 51:6, 7 (*lumen genti*).

108. Note the universalism that pervades this composition.

109. Flusser misses *stichos* 9; hence, his line numbers are misleading. The "faithful one" is David.

110. Or "high-officials."

111. Heb. תבל; usually means "world." The thought echoes the poetry in Ps 24:1, "The earth is the LORD's and all its fullness, the world and those who dwell therein."

112. Lit. "Adam."

113. For this expression, see Pss 71:16, 145:12, and 150:2.

114. סוף in biblical Hebrew means "end" and in Early Judaism obtains the meaning "mystery." Note the importance of mystery and secret in 1QpHab 7 and 1QH^a (*passim*).

115. Such universalism cannot be found among the Qumran compositions.

116. A reference back to those mentioned in line 10.

117. Lit. "will know."

For your hand, O Lord, has been doing all these things."[118]

Thanksgivings

13 Let the righteous one rejoice for he sees[119] these (things),
   And exults before you with chants and thanksgivings.[120]

14 May all the dwellers of the inhabited-world learn from me;[121]
   Then they will return to your way and worship[122] you in
       faithfulness.

15 And they will approach your face with thanks,
   With melodies[123] and chants and thanksgivings.[124]

16 They will magnify your glory in the midst of their camps;[125]
   And may they know that you, O Lord, created them.

The End of Idolatry

17 And all worshippers of (any) idol[126] will be shamed;[127]
   For they will become wise (perceiving them only)[128] as statues.

---

118. Flusser missed line 12. "A prayer of David" is extant in vv. 6–12.

119. A Hebrew imperfect.

120. Perhaps the poet alludes to the tradition that David chanted and danced when the ark was brought to Jerusalem. See Seow, *Myth, Drama, and the Politics of David's Dance*. See also 1 Chr 13:5–8.

121. "Me" refers to the one who has the vision, David.

122. Lit. "work" or "serve." See 1.8, 11.

123. Often with this noun the melody of a musical instrument is intended. See Isa 51:3 and Ps 81:3. See notably 1 Chr 13:8.

124. See Ps 95:2.

125. See Deut 23:10–15.

126. The Hebrew noun may denote an image of an idol, a symbol.

127. See 1.27 and Ps 97:7.

128. Note the cryptic nature of the ancient Hebrew poetry.

18 They will not continue to worship (false) gods;[129]
   And they will no longer bow down to the works of their (own) hands.

19 Then the (false) gods will completely disappear.[130]
   Their (idolatrous) delights[131] will be destroyed[132] utterly.[133]

Rejoicing in God's Wonderful Deeds

20 And you will be magnified and sanctified from the mouth of all your creatures[134]
   From now and forever.

21 For your servant (David) will recount your wonderful deeds,[135]
   According to his power and the spirit of his words.

22 For he has no joy in anything,[136]
   Except (in) your words and the appearance of your glory.[137]

23 Do not hide from me your multitude of mercies;
   And do not allow me to perish[138] for the sake of their love.

---

129. Or "idols."

130. An echo from Isa 2:18 and 20 according to 1QIsaᵃ and LXX (not the MT).

131. The author has written a sentence that should not suggest the idols are delightful or precious (the meaning of the Hebrew noun).

132. *Piel* imperfect.

133. The noun לנצח means "forever" or "for eternity"; but in the context of the parallel thought it means "utterly."

134. Lit. "works."

135. A quotation of Ps 75:2[1].

136. For this author David is alive and eternally present.

137. A clear echo from Exod 24:17; cf. Sir 49:8.

138. Lit. "die."

24 For I love the dwelling of your house[139]
   Above[140] all the shrines of kings.[141]

25 Better for me (is) the teaching[142] of your mouth,
   Than thousand of thousands of disks of gold.[143]

26 Better for me (is) your holy Word,
   Above delightful vessels.

27 Better for me (are) the commandments of your will above all precious[144] stones,
   And pearls,[145] the desires of kings.

Col. 3

Beatitude

1 Fully joyful is the one who finds glory in the desires of your will.
  And on account of you I, thus, I wish (something) from you,[146]

2 And this (is) my desire above all my requests:
  That I may live before you constantly,

3 And may I walk continuously[147] in your righteousness without iniquity;

---

139. See Ps 26:8 and Ps 84:2.
140. Lit. "from."
141. The poet refers to God's house, the Temple in Jerusalem. The echoes from Psalm 84 are obvious.
142. Heb. "Torah."
143. An echo of Ps 119:72.
144. Lit. "good."
145. Not a biblical Hebrew noun.
146. Lit. "from your face."
147. Read a *hitpael* imperfect.

Has Psalm 156 Been Found?

And may I pursue your truth every day,[148] as is right in your eyes.

4 Do not hold from me (what) I wish;
   And fulfill[149] my request according to the desires of your will.[150]

5 I will stand by them[151] unto eternity,
   To know all the paths of your righteousness.

Blessings

6 Blessed (is) God, who does this;
   Blessed (is) he, who performs all these (things).

7 Blessed (is) he who chose his servant (David);[152]
   And accomplishes all the wishes of my heart.[153]

8 Blessed (is) the name of the glory of his kingdom forever.[154]
   Blessed (is) the name of his glory to eternity and ever.

9 Blessed (is) the LORD God of Israel[155] from eternity and unto eternity.[156]
   And all the people said: "Amen."[157]

---

148. See Ps 86:11.

149. Lit. "do" or "make."

150. Cf. 11Q5 24.4–5. Also see Jesus's prayer in the garden of Gethsemane: "yet not what I will, but what you will" (Mark 14:36).

151. The reference is back to "the desires of your will" (line 4).

152. See Isa 43:10 (not David as God's servant).

153. As in other Semitic texts a poet shifts between first-person discourse and third-person discourse.

154. Cf. the numerous references to God's Kingdom by Jesus from Nazareth.

155. Obviously not Qumran's thought.

156. Lit. "from the eternity unto the eternity."

157. The poet echoes Ps 72:18–20. See also 2.4 and 4.15.

Translation of MS RNL Antonin 798

Second Vision (Concerning David's Vision of His Success and Treasures)[158]

10 On the third (day) in the month of Iyyar,
   I (David) saw in a vision all[159] his prophecies.[160]
   And I[161] prayed constantly[162] before the Lord and I said:[163]

11 "Blessed be the One[164] who bequeaths and makes rich.[165]
   Blessed be the One who causes falling and rising.[166]

12 For he lifts up the helpless one;[167]
   And from the ash-pits he rises up the poor one.[168]

13 And he magnified his (David's) throne[169] above all princes.
   And he made mighty his power above all rulers.

---

158. Stec, *The Genizah Psalms*; and Philomenko and Marx, "Quatres 'Chants' Pseudo-Davidiques" imagined a new psalm begins here.

159. Lit. "and all."

160. See 2.5.

161. David's words.

162. *Hitpael* imperfect.

163. Lines 11–12 echo the Prayer of Hannah in 1 Sam 2:7–8 that some Jews imagined was composed by David. Two prayers by Hannah begin 1 Samuel; two prayers by David close 2 Samuel. An *inclusio* is provided by 1 Samuel 2 (a chant of Hannah) and 2 Samuel 22 (a chant of David). Line 13 echoes this prayer. First Samuel 2:8 is paraphrased by Ps 113:7–9 (which is a Psalm of David). See also Luke 1:52.

164. I.e., "God."

165. See *Ps-Philo* celebration of Hannah's Prayer in chs. 50–51.

166. Note the four *hiphil* participles; others follow.

167. Eschatology (the claim that all God's promises will soon be fulfilled) appears only in the visions; elsewhere, we find the optimism created by the Maccabean and Hasmonean successes before about 105 BCE.

168. The author and the authors of the *Thanksgiving Hymns* use numerous words for "the poor": "the helpless" (דל), "the poor" (אביון), "the needy" (עני), and "the downcast" (רש). These nouns often denote metaphorical, not necessarily, economic plights.

169. See 2 Sam 7:16 and 1 Chr 17:12.

Has Psalm 156 Been Found?

14 And he gave to him all the delights[170] of kings,
  And the wealth of Gentiles[171] and treasures of kings,

15 Daughters of kings for his glory,
  And daughters of Jerusalem for the beauty of his kingdom.[172]

16 His joyfulness all worlds will declare.
  And before him all the resistances of the land will bow.

17 And they will trust in the LORD because of his great deeds.[173]
  And they will not err again with vanity[174] and horror.[175]

18 For all of them will know the LORD,[176]
  From the greatest ones of the human[177] and unto the smallest ones of the human.[178]

19 For the LORD judges through all the world,[179]
  One he causes to fall and one he allows to rise.[180]

---

170. See 1.21; 2.19, 26. "Desire" is represented by חפץ; see 1.6; 3.1, 2, 4.

171. See 2.16. In a vision, David sees his own throne and how the LORD gave him the delights of kings and the wealth of Gentiles.

172. See esp. 1 Chr 14:3. Notice how the author ignores David's adultery and murder of Uriah.

173. Lit. "for he magnified to do." See Ps 126:2–3 for the same phrase.

174. Or "with idols."

175. Or "desolation." The root is שמם, *polel*, "devastation," "horror." See Ezek 5:15, Joel 2:20–21, 4Q216 2.15.

176. Not a Qumran belief.

177. Lit. "Adam."

178. Cf. Ps 151A.

179. See Ps 58:12 and 94:2. According to David's psalm in 1 Chr 16:33, the LORD "is coming to judge the land (הארץ)." Has our poet shifted "land" (or "earth") to "world?"

180. Note the two *hipil* forms and the causative meaning. Is the author suggesting predestination (cf. Qumran)?

TRANSLATION OF MS RNL ANTONIN 798

20 To whom is wanting he shall give the inheritance;[181]
   And to the poor ones of the human[182] he shall allow to possess.

21 For in his hand (is) the living-being[183] of all life.
   And the spirit of all flesh to him, will bow."[184]

Exhortations to Worship[185]

22 O, chant to him; O, play a melody[186] to him.
   Ponder all his wonders.[187]

23 O, chant to his name in each appointed time,[188]
   For to him is befitting beauty and strength,
24 Who saves from trouble the living-being[189] of his beloved ones,
   And from the hand of all evil doers the spirit of his loyal ones.[190]

25 For he[191] trusted in his name and in the glory of the vision,[192]
   And in his[193] holy words and in all the ways of life.

26 Forever we will worship his (God's) name.

    181. See Num 27:11.
    182. Lit. "Adam."
    183. Heb. נפש.
    184. Lit. "they will bow." A second prayer of David is extant in vv. 11–21.
  185. If the poem was chanted by a priest in the Temple to glorify David, the exhortation would be by those chanting after him. The whitewashing of David's story is typical of postexilic thought (cf. Chronicles and Sirach).
  186. See 2.5; זמר often means "to play a melody on an instrument." See also Ps 105:2.
    187. An echo of 1 Chr 13:8 and a quotation of Ps 105:2 and 1 Chr 16:9.
    188. Heb. עת.
    189. Heb. נפש.
    190. Notice the plurals. An echo of Job 12:10.
    191. I.e. "David."
    192. See 2.5 and 3.10 for מראה.
    193. The pronoun refers to the LORD (see line 19).

And to the endtime of Endtimes we will tell of his might.

Col. 4

The Lord's Holiness

1. For he (the Lord)[194] is the one who heals those of a broken[195] heart.
   And he is the one who bandages[196] the bone(s) of the oppressed ones.

2. And he is the one who transforms aching to rejoicing,
   And shaking and trembling to great trustfulness.

3. For to him is the earth and (its) fullness,
   The world and those dwelling on it.[197]

4. For from before him he appointed his servant (David),[198]
   (With) splendor, and majesty,[199] and the glory of his kingdom.[200]

5. (The Lord) desires the good of his people.
   And he sent the one who heals and he healed their flesh.

6. And he (God) glorified his teaching through the mouth of his servant (David).
   And the commandment of his Word through the hands of his faithful one.[201]

---

194. I.e., God the Lord.
195. A plural.
196. Heb. וחבש.
197. Perhaps the scribe forgot to copy the final *he*. Note the echoes from Ps 24:1 (a Psalm of David).
198. I.e., David.
199. See Ps 21:6.
200. Perhaps the poet identifies God's kingdom with David's kingdom.
201. I.e., David.

7 He (David) increased in his heart wisdom[202] and discernment;
And the multitude of his holiness exceeds recounting.

The Incomparable Mercies of the LORD

8 Who resembles him and who is like him?[203]
He who did not forget the cry of the poor one.[204]

9 And he (the LORD) remembered in his mercies the needy and helpless.
And I remembered[205] the strengths, and might of his kingdom, and beauty of his strength.

10 Night and day I stand before him.
And I bless his memory above all his works.[206]

11 Be blessed and be exalted, O Lord[207] of all the generations.
Be holy and be glorified,[208] O Ruler in all his works.

12 You are unique,[209] O my King,[210] according to the utterance of all your worshipers.[211]

---

202. See 1.6.

203. See the *Self-Glorification Hymn*. The referent may be David who did not "forget the cry of the poor one." David conflates with "God" in MS RNL Antonin 798.

204. A quotation from Ps 9:13, "He did not forget the cry of the afflicted;" LXX: "forget not the poor ones" (τῶν πενήτων; 9:12).

205. Through transmission the beginning of this *stichos* was considered the end of 9a.

206. Note the following string of plural nouns.

207. Heb. אדון.

208. There are four verbs in the *hitpael* form (a reflexive).

209. Another *hitpael*. Perhaps the monotheism of Second Isaiah is reflected. Possibly: "you are one" and a vague allusion to the Shema of Deut 6:4.

210. I.e., the LORD.

211. Lit. "servants."

Has Psalm 156 Been Found?

O Judge of Righteousness and Defender[212] of Truth.

Blessings

13 Blessed are you, O LORD God; may he remember in his mercies[213]
The covenant of his servant[214] for eternity.[215]

14 Blessed be the glorious name of his kingdom for ever and ever.
Blessed be his glorious name for ever and ever.

15 Blessed be the LORD, the God of Israel from eternity and unto eternity;
And let all the people say: "Amen."[216]

Third Vision (Concerning David's Praise of the LORD, "The Judge")[217]

16 On the fourth (day) in the month of Iyyar,
In the spirit, I (David) saw in the Holy vision[218] and all his prophecies.[219]

---

212. Another noun for "judge." See Ps 68:6.

213. See the Beatitudes in the First Vision (col. 2) in which the author refers to the LORD God.

214. David is the "servant." See 1.15.

215. The celebration of God's eternal covenant with David is without messianic overtones. This may indicate a date of composition closer to 200 BCE than 100 BCE. See the celebration of David's eternal covenant in the Psalm of David cited in 1 Chr 16:13–17. Also see David's last words according to 2 Sam 23:5. Cf. Ps 89:40.

216. See the note to 2.4. The poet quotes Ps 106:48.

217. Stec, *The Genizah Psalms*; and Philomenko and Marx, "Quatres 'Chants' Pseudo-Davidiques" imagined a fourth psalm begins here.

218. Only here does the author refer to "the Holy Vision." His thought develops through this psalm. See Stec: "in the spirit I considered the holy vision"; ctr. Flusser and Safrai: "I beheld a vision"; Philonenko and Marx: "je vis en esprit, dans une vision, la Sainteté."

219. For this formula, see 2.5 and 3.10.

Translation of MS RNL Antonin 798

And I prayed constantly before the Lord and I said:

17 "Blessed (be the Lord),[220] for he has broken the wicked ones,
And caused to stand the horn[221] of the righteous ones.[222]

18 And his knowledge and his wisdom fill[223] my heart,
For you are the Judge of righteousness.[224]

19 And a false[225] judgment shall not go out from before you,
But only truth and faithfulness.

20 You will repay[226] to the human[227] according to his ways,
And according to the fruits of his evil-practices[228] you will return to him.

21 There is no deceitfulness in all your works.
And there is no deception[229] in all your words.

22 All your doing (is) perfect together.[230]
And perversity will never be found[231] in your work.

---

220. Again, note how cryptic ancient Hebrew can be.
221. For "horn," see David's song in 2 Sam 22:3, "the horn of my salvation."
222. Note the echo from Ps 75:11 (a Psalm of Asaph).
223. Lit. "(is) in all my heart."
224. See 1.2.
225. Lit. "lying."
226. Lit. "to give."
227. Lit. "Adam." Adam represents the human. All will be judged by "The Judge."
228. The text echoes Jer 17:10; cf. also Isa 3:10, Jer 2:14, and 32:19.
229. Or "lie." There is no fraud in god's judgments or works.
230. The use of יחד is pre-Qumranic. Note the two singular nouns in line 22.
231. *Niphal* imperfect.

23 Like a flooding river you increased[232] your judgment;
And like a blessed seed you caused to grow your righteousness."

Beatitude and Promise

24 Fully joyful is the one purified[233] by your holiness;
He will recount your glory during each day.

25 I was helped[234] from the presence of your glory,[235]
To be able for eternity to stand by your will.

26 For the day (is) comple[ted]:
Fully joyful are those who keep your commands.[236]

Summary

Notice the refined poetry intermittently in this Psalm. The form is almost always *parallelismus membrorum*, and I have arranged the English to reflect that poetic form so well known to all who read the Davidic Psalter and the preceding pages. A good example of the presentation in bicolon poetry that is synonymous is 1.4–5:

---

232. Lit. "multiply."

233. Or "cleansed." See the famous Ps 51:6[4] which is defined as a Psalm of David, who confesses his adultery with Bathsheba, an episode that is noticeably absent in MS RNL Antonin 798.

234. Or "helped" by becoming stronger. Note the echo from Ps 28:7. See the poem by Amasai, when some of the sons of Benjamin and Judah joined David, whom God helped (עזר) according to 1 Chr 12:18.

235. See 11QPs^a 27.11, in which David speaks as a prophet "from before the Most High." Also see Acts 2:29–30 (Δαυὶδ ... προφήτης οὖν ὑπάρχων). Stec draws attention to Rabbinics in which David is acknowledged to be a prophet (*b. Sotah* 48b). See also the *Targum on the Psalms* (18:1, 49:12, 103:1) and 2 Sam 23:2. The *Pesharim* on Davidic Psalms indicate that some Qumranites assumed David was a prophet.

236. Notice "commands," "instructions," or "precepts," but these are not necessarily "Torah."

4 And you divided the world between darkness and light,
   And between impurity and purity and between falsehood and righteousness.

5 You cast off from your people all the sons of foreigners;
   And you purified your flock from impure beasts.

The first bicolon is synonymous: darkness is parallel to impurity and falsehood, but light is parallel to purity and righteousness. Then the synonymous parallelism is repeated: "your people" are "your flock" and "all the sons of foreigners" are "impure beasts." Such perception of poetry helps comprehend the meaning of words and the thought pattern of early Jews. The poetry is scripted in bicola from 1.1 to 2.4, which is the conclusion of beatitudes and the appearance of the first vision. The first apparent tricolon may be in 2.5, but there the poetry is introduced by the identification of the month and day. Arrangement in bicola continue until 3.10, which is also the introduction of the month and day. Again, the poetry is presented in bicola until 4.16, which is, as before, a tricolon with the introduction of the month and day. Bicola continue until the end of the psalm (as extant). Thus, it is obvious that the poet constructed his psalm with bicola, a few tricola, and *parallelismus membrorum*.

We have seen an acrostic in the Hebrew of Psalm 155:9–13. A partial acrostic is also clear in 1.1—2.1; but the order is not perfect. Insightful and new is the observation concerning orthography—that is, final consonants are considered different from their corresponding consonant in an initial or medial position.

Is MS RNL Antonin 798 a "Psalm of David"?

What makes an ancient psalm a "Psalm of David"? Those who answer too quickly should double-check the psalms in the Davidic Psalter.[237] Not all are attributed to "David." Some are attributed

237. Karel van der Toorn argues that Psalm 20 was originally an Egyptian psalm edited by an Egyptian Jew who added Messianic ideologies in the third

to Solomon, as for example, Psalm 72 ("Of Solomon"); yet Psalm 72:20 concludes as follows: "End of the Psalms of David, son of Jesse."

Many Psalms have no attribution, as with Psalms 1–2 and 112–119, or are attributed to "the sons of Korah," as in Psalms 42 and 44–49. Many Psalms have "To the Chief Musician," sometimes with "of the Sons of Korah," "A Psalm of David," or "A Psalm of Asaph." The superscript for Psalms 120–134 is "A Chant of Ascents," but the phrase is of uncertain meaning. Many other psalms, notably Psalms 124, 131, and 133, have the addition "Of David;" but Psalms 72 and 127 have "Of Solomon." Manuscripts preserving what are potentially "Davidic Psalms" frequently have lost an attribution, and some of them are attributed to Moses, as in Psalm 90. As we have seen with Psalms 154 and 155 in Syriac, the attribution is to "Hezekiah," who did not even live during David's time and was not heralded as a composer of psalms.

David is not mentioned in the poetry of Psalms 151–155. In contrast to these non-Masoretic Psalms and many psalms attributed to David in the Davidic Psalter, David is mentioned in this Non-Masoretic Psalm, ostensibly Psalm 156. Here are the references in col. 1:

15 You made a pledge ahead to David your servant,
   And you anointed with compassion the Shoot of Jesse.

16 You sustained his arm through your holiness,
   For he established your praise unto the ends of the earth.

17 (As) an eternal pillar you set his name.
   And he is breaking through the wall and rebuilding the ruins.

18 (David is) a cornerstone despised which the builders despised,
   And you raised (him) to be head above all the nations.

---

century BCE. See van der Toorn, "Celebrating the New Year with the Israelites," 633–49. As is well known, in the canon Psalm 20 has this attribution: "For the Leader. A Psalm of David."

Translation of MS RNL Antonin 798

19 Magnificence and a crown you have allowed him to inherit with rejoicing.
And the splendor of all the Gentiles you are calling his name.

20 Righteousness and justice you multiplied in his (David's) days.
And peace and blessings forever without number.

In addition to these explicit references to David, the second-person pronoun, "me," and the third-person pronoun, "he" or "him," sometimes refers to David; this is done either by the author or by many who read this psalm and considered it a Psalm of David. The following verses are probably meant to refer to David; they follow after verse 20, just quoted:

21 All the elect ones of righteousness shout for joy before you (David),
For they will be happy in the pleasant land.

22 You made holy through his (David's) mouth the name of the Great One (God).
And the chants of your strength he recounts each day.

23 Above all the angels you (O God) made his (David's) greatness.
And king of all the nations you placed him for eternity.

24 You broke before him all the kings of Midian.
And you drowned in the depths those who hate him.

25 You supported his right arm over his sword.
And you strengthened his arm over the mighty-warriors of Kedar.

26 His leg will not stagger for he trusted through your name.
And his power will not stumble for you helped him through love.

The pronouns "you," "his," "him," and "he" often are intended for David. In MS RNL Antonin 798, except for "Adam" in 4.20, which probably means "human," only two nouns are identified: they are "LORD" (that is, "God") or "David." Hence, the indefinite pronouns, so typical of Semitics, either refer to God or David; and perhaps we should ponder a *double entente*.

The reference to the "kings of Midian" has no association with David. It is narratively linked with Moses (see Exod 2-4, 18 and Num 25, 31). The latest reference to Midian as a political entity is found in Gen 36:35 and may be dated to 1100 BCE.[238] The author attributes to David victories earlier associated with Moses and Joshua.

The mention of "the mighty-warriors of Kedar" does not help us with identifying individuals in our Psalm because the reference has no connection in traditions with David. Kedar is the most powerful North Arabian tribe; but its most influential time was long after David, or from the eighth century to the fourth century BCE. The most important references to Kedar in the Old Testament signify something despicable and a cause of woe (see Gen 25:13, Ps 120:5, Isa 21:16-17, Jer 2:10, Ezek 27:21; see also Pliny the Elder, *NH* 5.11[12], 65).[239]

The most important reference to David is in 1.23. While it is well known that David was heralded as a prophet in antiquity, especially from the attributions in Hebrew and especially in the Aramaic (the Targumim) of Psalms 14, 18, 103 and in the Targumim of Ps 49:16,[240] Ps 156 1.23 quite startlingly claims that David is "above the angels" and "king" for "eternity." Recall that line:

> Above all the angels you (O God) made his (David's) greatness.
> And king of all the nations you placed him for eternity.

In the future the exalted status of Enoch, Melchizedek, the person of the *Self-Glorification Hymn*, Moses, Solomon, the Righteous Teacher, Hillel, Jesus, and Paul needs to be rethought.[241]

238. See Knauf, Μαδιάμα, 16-21; and Mendenhall, "Midian," 815-18.
239. I am indebted to the superb work of Knauf, "Kedar," 9-10.
240. See esp. Evans, "The Reputation of Jesus," 629-51.
241. The secondary literature on this research is excessive; see esp. Hurtado, *One God, One Lord*; Dunn, *Jesus and the Spirit*; Smith, "Two Ascended

Translation of MS RNL Antonin 798

With the insights and perceptions obtained in chapter 2, we may now ask whether MS RNL Antonin 79 should be renamed. Is it not like Psalms 151–155? Should it be acknowledged as "Psalm 156"?

---

into Heaven"; Hurtado, *Lord Jesus Christ*; Miller, "The Self-Glorification Hymn Reexamined"; Loke, *The Origin of Divine Christology*.

3

Has Psalm 156 Been Found?

The major focus of this monograph concerns the identity of MS RNL Antonin 798. Is it "Psalm 156"? In seeking to answer this question, we must employ the methodologies used for finding nomenclatures for the so-called Psalms of David 151–155. We need to discern if the "Psalm" is a medieval composition or if it was composed before the codification of the Mishnah shortly after 200 CE.

Can we discover if the "Psalm" is Davidic in any way—that is, is David mentioned or considered the author? In exploring this issue, we should not forget that the psalms in the Davidic Psalter are not consistently attributed to David, that Psalms 151–155, especially Psalms 154 and 155 in Syriac, are attributed to Hezekiah, and that the beginning of the Hebrew of Psalm 155 (11QPs[a] 155) is lost.

In the following pages I will share my observations obtained while preparing a critical introduction, text, and translation of this impressive psalm that may be labeled "Psalm 156." Along with most specialists, I have become convinced that this psalm which was found in the Cairo Genizah should be included among the collection of documents found in the Qumran caves.[1] It is not a medieval composition; like the *Damascus Document* and the

---

1. It will be included, in an appendix, in PTSDSSP 9A.

Has Psalm 156 Been Found?

Aramaic Testament of Levi, the psalm was probably taken to Cairo from the Qumran caves about 800 CE. It has become clear that a majority of scholars who have worked on the psalm discern that it was probably once deposited in caves near Jericho, and that designation probably means the Qumran caves.

Research on MS RNL Antonin 798 has been restricted because of four factors. First, the early work appeared in inaccessible and virtually unknown publications, and the initial publication was placed in the unfamiliar *HaGoren* by a specialist in Gaonic Arabic. Second, the popular work by David Flusser and Samuel Safrai does not reach the level of excellence of these distinguished experts in Early Judaism; some of their mistakes have misled some experts. Third, the constant references to "the Genizah Psalms" imply that the psalm is medieval and not important for scholars focused on Early Judaism and Christian Origins. Fourth, the psalm has not been placed in any known collection, and the text and translation are not widely known. As Meir Bar-Ilan reported, "the speculative nature of the discussions makes it clear that the historical circumstances and contexts of the entire issue from its very beginnings require further clarification."[2] In the following, I intend to remove the weakly speculative dimensions of work on this psalm.

As we explore the provenience and meaning of MS RNL Antonin 798, now in the National Library in Saint Petersburg, five issues for discussion should be brought into focus. First, how many psalms are preserved in the medieval manuscript; is it one or as many as four? If four, why is a month mentioned just before a vision, and why is there no *incipit* or something like "a Psalm of David" or an opening like "O Lord, I called unto you" (Psalm 155 [11QPs^a 155])? Second, what is the date of this Psalm; is it prior to the second century BCE, prior to 40 BCE, or prior to 70 CE? Third, is this psalm "Davidic"; is David mentioned in the psalm, and is he the speaker and the one who has the vision? Fourth, what is the relation of this psalm to Qumran; was it composed at Qumran or taken to Qumran from somewhere else, perhaps Jerusalem? Fifth, should this psalm be known as "Psalm 156"?

2. Bar-Ilan, "Non-Canonical Psalms from the Genizah," 703.

Has Psalm 156 Been Found?

The Hebrew Leather Manuscript

Preserved on two leather pages, written on both sides, and of 27 lines (cols. 1 and 2) or 26 lines (cols. 3 and 4), is a psalm composed in imitation of the Psalter and in a type of Hebrew influenced by the Psalter but using personal license.[3] The manuscript may be dated between the eighth and tenth centuries CE. The tenth century seems to be the latest possible date for the manuscript. Its paleography is similar to the Egyptian manuscripts with a square script.[4] The 'aleph is strikingly similar to the forms in the eighth-century scroll of 1 Kings (fig. 103 in Yardeni, *The Book of Hebrew Script*). The *bet* is similar to the forms in the eighth-century Genesis scroll (fig. 97). The elongated 'ayin is similar to the types found in the eighth-century Genesis scroll and also in the tenth-century "Zadokite Document" (fig. 99). The elegant scribal hand of Psalm 156 seems also, at times, a mirror image of a pre-70 Qumran scroll, so early forms may be caused by copying.[5]

How Many Psalms are Preserved in MS RNL Antonin 798?

Now we may entertain our first question: How many psalms are found in this manuscript? David Flusser and Samuel Safrai refer to

---

3. Perhaps Bar-Ilan assumes too unified a standard for biblical Hebrew when he stated that the author "wrote poetry in his own personal style, idiosyncratic and unusual, and not biblical in any aspect" ("Non-Canonical Psalms from the Genizah," 697). I judge with others like Flusser and Safrai that the poet is influenced by biblical Hebrew. His words also mirror postbiblical Hebrew with the complex mixture of Aramaic and proto-Rabbinic forms. Some passages are well crafted and full of symbolic language; other passages are not in good Hebrew, resulting in faulty compositions and copying over one thousand years and without the interlinear scribal corrections and other improvements obvious in most manuscripts found in the eleven Qumran caves. Some of these errors can be attributed to the many stages in copying the text. See further: E. Fleischer, "Medieval Hebrew Poems in Biblical Style," 207-24.

4. See Yardeni, *The Book of Hebrew Script*, 80-83.

5. I am appreciative of the information and insights shared in Lorein and van Staalduine-Sulman, "Songs of David," 257-71; see esp. p. 257.

"psalms" in this section of a much larger composition, but do not clarify how many they discern, and no evidence can be found in their translation (see below). David M. Stec thought the work was composed of three and one-third psalms.[6]

Flusser and Safrai argued that the transitions they perceived, separating the psalms preserved in this work, were marked by three "doxological statements" or "transition" statements that imitate the concluding verses of the biblical Psalter.[7] These transitions in Psalm 156 are highlighted by "Amen" (in italics) and are as follows:

First:

> Blessed is the name of his glory for ever and ever.
> Blessed is the LORD, the God of Israel, from eternity and (unto) eternity.
> And all the people said; "*Amen.*" (2.3)

Second:

> Blessed (is) the name of the glory of his kingdom forever.
> Blessed (is) the name of his glory to eternity and ever.
>
> Blessed (is) the LORD God of Israel from eternity and unto eternity.
> And all the people said: "*Amen.*" (3.8–9)

Third:

> Blessed be the LORD, the God of Israel, from eternity and unto eternity;
> And let all the people say, "*Amen.*" (4.15)

The third blessing is almost the exact conclusion to the fourth book of the Psalter (Ps 106:48; see this verse below). It also resembles the ending of the first book of the Psalter (Ps 41:14). These blessings are similar to other section endings in the Psalter; note the following:

---

6. Stec, *The Genizah Psalms*, 4.
7. Flusser and Safrai, "The Apocryphal Psalms of David," 268.

Has Psalm 156 Been Found?

End of Psalm 72:

> Blessed is the LORD God, God of Israel,
> Who alone does wondrous things;
> Blessed is His glorious name forever;
> His glory fills the whole world.
> Amen and Amen.

End of the prayers of David son of Jesse. [Ps 72:18–20 JPS TANAKH]

End of Psalm 106:48 (cf. Ps 156 4.15):

> Blessed is the LORD, God of Israel,
> From eternity to eternity.
> Let all the people say, "Amen."
> Hallelujah [JPS TANAKH]

There is some wisdom in the conclusion by Flusser and Safrai that the three doxological statements are an imitation of the concluding verses of the Davidic Psalter.[8] Without any doubt, our author memorized the Psalter and crafted his work from such verses as those just quoted.

Unfortunately, Flusser and Safrai did not clarify their insight about the existence of more than one psalm in this manuscript, and their comments are vague, even confusing.[9] Perhaps they imagined there were (at least portions of) four psalms extant. It is certain that many more psalms were once contained in this collection. Their discovery seems forced, but it influenced Stec and all the others who began with their publication. The "Amen" may not begin a new psalm, and those worshiping are not called to chant it on successive days; the days of Iyyar mentioned serve to highlight the visions.

---

8. Ibid. I find it difficult to follow them at all points, but the influence from the Psalter is certain.

9. Ibid.

HAS PSALM 156 BEEN FOUND?

Are there about four psalms in MS RNL Antonin 798?[10] Flusser and Safrai might be correct in perceiving numerous psalms in MS RNL Antonin 798. As stated, these scholars have influenced subsequently all who work on this text. In favor of their insight is the fact that the Davidic Psalter "Amen" ends a psalm (see 41:13, 72:19, 89:52, 106:48).

If the blessings are "three doxological statements" to demarcate the end or beginning of a psalm, then we should note that 3.6–9 is a list of blessings (and then the second vision is given). Then, a second list of blessings is found in 4.13–15 (and then the third vision commences).

An answer should follow careful reflections. "Amen" appears in the first "transition." While "Amen" can end a psalm (e.g., Psalm 106), it can also indicate liturgically the time when "the people" are to join in voice with the officiating priest. For example, this kind of "Amen" occurs in and commences the *Rule of the Community*. See 1QS 1.20 [*bis*], 2.10 [*bis*], 2.18 [*bis*]. Most importantly, in our text, "Amen" is used to introduce "a vision" (2.5, 3.10; cf. 4.16), and the flow of thought does not clarify the beginning of a new psalm. The refrain is, "and all the people said: 'Amen.'" Thus, the "Amen" functions precisely as the *Pisqah be'meṣaʿ pasuq* ("a sectional division in the middle of a verse") in the Hebrew Bible, allowing the Jews worshiping in the Temple to fill in a caesura, perhaps even reciting, as Talmon claimed, Psalm 151.[11] The use of "Amen" in our psalm seems reminiscent of the abundant use of "Amen" in Deut 27:15–26. The use of "Amen" in documents found in the Qumran caves does not end psalms or prayers; see especially 4Q286 frg. 7a col. 2b–d lines 1, 5, 6, and 10. Some Jewish prayers have "Amen" not at the end but during the psalm or prayer. Finally, it seems odd to begin a new psalm with "In the month of Iyyar . . ." (2.5, 3.10, 4.16). The "Amen" probably introduces a vision, not a new psalm.

---

10. Bar-Ilan judged that the work contained "four hymns or psalms," but correctly referred to the psalm as "a liturgical piece." Bar-Ilan, "Non-Canonical Psalms from the Genizah," 697.

11. Talmon, "Extra-Canonical Hebrew Psalms from Qumran—Psalm 151," 264–72.

Thus, it seems likely the visions are part of one psalm and are anticipated by the people saying "Amen." The difference between the view of Flusser and Safrai and our view would then be between four psalms and one long psalm with sections devoted to David's visions.

Even though we must allow for some verses to have become lost,[12] our psalm is not too long to define one psalm. It contains a total of 106 verses while Psalm 119 in the Davidic Psalter preserves 176 verses.

We are left with a major question: Does the manuscript preserve one long psalm with three instances of "Amen" (2.4, 3.9, 4.15), which is found always before a vision? Is "Amen" a call for those in the Temple to chant: "Amen"? Does this exclamation end a psalm or demarcate a section of one psalm and introduce three visions attributed to David? Is the presentation similar to 4Q525 in which a *vacat* often separates beatitudes? I am convinced, but willing to be persuaded I am wrong, that "Amen" introduces a vision and not a new psalm.

Date and Provenience

Experts have offered their judgments about the origins of MS RNL Antonin 798. In chronological order, they are as follows:

- 1902 Harkavy assumed the Psalm was composed in the Middle Ages (perhaps by David Alroi or Abraham Abulafia),[13] but he could not know what we have learned since 1947.

- 1982 (2007) Flusser and Safrai concluded the work may have originated at Qumran.[14]

---

12. Flusser and Safrai claimed that our psalm mentions "the first, second, third and fourth of Iyar" (Flusser and Safrai, "The Apocryphal Psalms of David,"266); but the "first" is lost.

13. Harkavy in *Ha-Goren*, 82–85.

14. Flusser and Safrai, "The Apocryphal Psalms of David," 265–67.

Has Psalm 156 Been Found?

1991 Fleischer opined that the text postdates the Arab conquest of the seventh century.[15]

1996 Haran claimed, without detailed research, that the work originates with the Karaites.[16]

1997 Philonenko and Marx judged this work to be a Qumran composition.[17]

2005 Lorein and Van Staalduine-Sulman concluded the work is from Qumran.[18]

2011 Bar-Ilan dated this psalm "a century or so after the destruction" of 70 CE.[19]

2013 Stec postulated that this composition antedated 68 CE and was composed in Palestine.

Those who glance at this list would probably conclude that there is no consensus and would agree with Bar-Ilan, who has published a brilliant and erudite study: "There is no agreement either on the provenience or the date of this text from the Genizah. The affiliation of the document with Qumran is debatable, and it is encircled by a cloud of hypotheses."[20]

---

15. Fleischer, "Medieval Hebrew Poems in Biblical Style," 207–24.

16. Haran, *The Biblical Collection*, 154–69.

17. Philonenko and Marx, "Quatre 'Chants' Pseudo-Davidiques," 385–406; see esp. p. 390.

18. They judge the document is from Qumran but very late because of the use of עולם. See Lorein and van Staalduine-Sulman, "A Song of David for Each Day," 33–59. Also see Lorein and van Staalduine-Sulman, "Songs of David," 257.

19. Bar-Ilan, "Non-Canonical Psalms from the Genizah," 708. He is impressed by the diversity of Judaism then in the third century CE; but such diversity antedates, not postdates, 70 CE. The importance of the Jewish sects and groups ends in 70 CE. Subsequently, within Judaism the dominant group is clearly the Pharisees. He is also impressed that "the slaughtered sheep" (from Ps 44:23) postdates 70 or 136 CE (p. 707). In Jewish liturgy the most appropriate date would indicate the desecration of the Temple by Antiochus Epiphanes in the second century BCE.

20. Bar-Ilan, "Non-Canonical Psalms from the Genizah," 696.

We may now contemplate our second question: What is the date of this psalm? If one concentrates upon the conclusions of those who focused research on this psalm, and notably upon those who have crafted a text and translation, a consensus does emerge. Flusser, Safrai, Philonenko, Marx, Lorein, van Staalduine-Sulman, Bar-Ilan, and Stec concur that the psalm dates from Early Judaism (300 BCE to 200 CE), and that the manuscript found in the Cairo Genizah is a copy of a much earlier document.

Despite Bar-Ilan's arguments, the consensus also entails the conclusion that the psalm antedates 70 CE and was composed in a Hebrew that often reflects the Hebrew Bible, since the author often reveals that he has memorized many passages now in the Psalter. A consensus does not mean universal agreement; it denotes that the majority of scholars who are qualified to make a judgment tend to agree. Stec has explored the provenience and date of our psalm, and his judgment deserves quoting:

> My own view is that all the evidence is consistent with an origin of the Genizah Psalms in about the 1st century CE, and that there are no linguistic features that would suggest or require a date later than the 2nd century. It seems likely to me that our psalms were composed in Palestine at about the same time, or slightly later than, the literature of Qumran.[21]

While many specialists will be in agreement with much that Stec has concluded,[22] it is also certain that the Qumran literature covered many centuries. It is also probable that our psalm was composed before 70 CE and conceivably earlier than 100 BCE, as I shall indicate.

The author either imagines or more likely experiences the joy of the cult in the Temple; note "For I love the dwelling of your house / Above all the shrines of kings" (2.24). The thought is an echo of Ps 84:1–2; but in the judgment of previous experts, the Temple cult was active when our poet composed this Psalm. If the reference to "the shrines of kings" is to be taken literally, then a

---

21. Stec, *The Genizah Psalms*, 22.
22. Notice how Stec rejects Bar-Ilan's dating.

time during the reign of King Herod or (better) Aristobulus I (c. 104–100) would be possible. Thus, the exhortation to worship reflects a time when the Temple was the center of worship (3.22–26). It is certain that the psalm made its way to the Cairo Genizah and is thus similar to the *Damascus Document*, the *Aramaic Testament of Levi*, and also conceivably to MS London-Ashkar of the seventh or eighth century CE, which also comes from Egypt.[23]

Despite the prominence and erudition of those who have worked on this psalm, no scholar has been impressed by the author's optimism and joy of driving out the idol worshipers and Gentiles from the Land of the Jews, the Holy Land. Many exultations could be dismissed as eschatological hopes that cannot be dated; but do they fit the social and historical setting—and the intellectual climate experienced by Jews—after 63 BCE when Pompey entered the Land and the Temple with force? Obviously, they must antedate 70 CE when Jerusalem was destroyed and the Temple burned. The thrill of having the heathen nations driven out of the Land seems mirrored in the following:

> God has "cast off from your people all the sons of foreigners" (1.5)
>
> "You planted righteous ones in the land of truth;
> And justice you multiplied throughout the world." (1.7)
>
> All the elect ones of righteousness shout for joy before you,
> For they are being happy in the delightful land. (1.21)

If the section on how God has purified and renewed the nation (1.5–12) is historical and not eschatological (as the visions), then it must antedate 63 BCE, when, according to Josephus, "we lost our freedom and became subject to the Romans" (*Ant.* 14.77). The author of the *Psalms of Solomon* castigates Pompey as that insolent infidel who smashed the fortified walls of Jerusalem with "his battering-ram" (2:1). The references to the glory of God's kingdom

---

23. See Engel and Mishor, "An Ancient Scroll of the Book of Exodus," 24–60; and Charlesworth, "Ashkar Manuscript 2," 66–69.

Has Psalm 156 Been Found?

(3.8; 4.4, 9, 14), obviously on earth, makes best sense among the Jews in Palestine before the Roman "conquest" of 63 BCE. The exhortation to worship because God saved his beloved ones and his loyal ones "from the hand of all evil doers" (3.24) reflects the spiritual climate after Simon's expulsion of the idolatrous Greeks (= the Seleucids) from the Acre, or citadel, contiguous to the Temple (1 Macc 13:49; *Ant.* 13.215). Then, for only a few years Simon brought "peace to the Land" (1 Macc 14:11) so that the Jews "prospered exceedingly and overcame the foes that surrounded them" (*War* 13.214).

The denigration of idol worship in 2.17–19 may well reflect the battles over idolatry by the Maccabees and the early Hasidim. The claim that the elect ones "will be happy in the delightful land" assumes that the Land of Israel is not being trampled under the feet of Greek or Roman soldiers. The hypothesis that this psalm dates between 165 and 63 BCE looks promising, but we should not be positivistic because this is a poem, and the successes of King David are intermixed with joyful expectations. Yet, no passages excerpted above are from the three visions, and the dreams attributed to David were experienced, if only intermittently, by the Hasmoneans. David Flusser and Samuel Safrai offer an attractive and compelling scenario. These pages preserving a Psalm of David

> are probably the remnants of a large apocryphal work composed during the Second Temple period, and that made its way from Qumran to the Genizah in the same way as did the Damascus Document and the Aramaic Testament of Levi, fragments of which were found at Qumran.[24]

Flusser and Safrai, two of the great scholars who taught in Jerusalem, were convinced that the Qumran *Psalms Scroll* (11Q5) knew our psalm:

> It is noteworthy that apparently the Psalms Scroll from Qumran not only mentions our composition, but it discusses the divine inspiration that rested upon David

---

24. Flusser and Safrai, "The Apocryphal Psalms of David," 258.

in his writing. The passage opens with the statement: "And David, son of Jesse, was wise, and a light like the light of the sun" (11Q5 27.2), while the Genizah psalms read "you have placed me in your might as a light to the nations" (2.8; based on Isaiah 42;6; 49:6). The Qumran psalms then state that "YHWH gave him a discerning and enlightened spirit' (11Q5 27.4), and conclude with the words, "All these [David] spoke through the spirit of prophecy which had been given to him from before the Most High" (11Q5 27.11).[25]

While I would like to affirm the hypothesis that the author of MS RNL Antonin 798 knew the Qumran *Psalms Scroll*, that conclusion has not been demonstrated; we can only be confident that the author of MS RNL Antonin 798 shared the same culture and time with the author or scribe of the *Psalms Scroll*, the *Self-Glorification Hymn*, and the *Testament of Judah*. Also not demonstrated is the conclusion by Flusser and Safrai that the verses in MS RNL Antonin 798 "were composed during the Second Temple period and were part of the same movement from which the Qumran community emerged."[26]

It is appropriate now to entertain our third question: What relation, if any, has our psalm to David? Is it a David Pseudepigraphon? Three visions are attributed to David (2.5–12, 3.10–21, and 4.16–23). The visions all occur in the month of Iyyar; perhaps the Psalm was related to others and contained readings for certain days. Thanksgivings, rejoicings, and blessings characterize the optimistic tone (2.13–16, 20–27; 3.6–9). Idol worship has ended (2.17–19). Signaled out for celebration is the LORD's graciousness (4.1–7) and his incomparable mercies (4.8–12). The poem preserves a partial acrostic: *gimel* to *taw* in 1.1–27. Since the beginning of the psalm is lost, it is possible that the beginning of the acrostic, accounting for letters ʾ*aleph* and *bet*, is also lost. However, it is possible that the beginning has been misplaced at the end (probably through scribal error during copying over the years);

---

25. Ibid., 267.
26. Ibid., 268–69.

though the *'aleph* and *bet* following the *taw* of this acrostic might be coincidental or may start another partial acrostic which was cut short. Additionally, the *ḥet* appeared for *he* in the acrostic, and many letters were repeated but in sequence and final forms were considered separate consonants.

Did early Jews develop an imagination whereby David was seen as a prophet who had visions? The extant *Pesharim*, Qumran compositions, are commentaries on Isaiah, Hosea, Micah, Nahum, Habakkuk, Zephaniah, and also the Davidic Psalms (4Q171, 1Q16, 4Q173); thus, the Qumranites, following other early Jews, most likely believed that David had prophetic powers. Jewish lore evolved so that David was clearly a prophet, as proved by notable documents such as *Sotah* 48b in the Babylonian Talmud, and the *Targum on the Psalms* (18:1, 49:17, 103:1).[27] MS RNL Antonin 798 is therefore a David Pseudepigraphon.

We may now explore our fourth question: What relation, if any, does our text have to Qumran? Most of the scholars who have devoted time to studying the manuscript in Saint Petersburg would agree that the composition is either from Qumran or was placed in a Qumran cave. I have no doubt that this psalm was taken to Qumran from elsewhere in ancient Palestine, as is the case with the vast number of scrolls found in Caves I–XI.

Stec reported that "no trace of our document was actually found at Qumran."[28] This statement would carry much weight if we had a large percentage of what had been in the eleven caves (and there may be more to report later); we have less than 10 percent of what was in the Qumran caves. Qumranologists point out that seven scrolls were found in Cave I, but more than seventy additional scrolls were left in fragments on the cave's floor. The Bedouin destroyed many scrolls. Moreover, Peter W. Flint concluded that we have only forty-nine of the original fifty-six psalms of David in the Qumran *Psalms Scroll* (11QPs^a).[29] While there is

---

27. See the insightful comments in Stec, *The Genizah Psalms*, 6. See the fuller discussion of David as a prophet in chapter 4.

28. Ibid., 4.

29. Flint, *The Dead Sea Scrolls and the Book of Psalms*, 172–201; and Flint,

Has Psalm 156 Been Found?

no evidence of this psalm at Qumran, we do not have a way of knowing all that was known at Qumran or even read there. Again, insightful are the thoughts of Flusser and Safrai:

> If these apocryphal psalms did in fact originate in the Qumran library, it may be that they simply did not survive though it is also possible that there were removed in their entirety and thus found their way into the hands of medieval Jews. If so, they simply were no longer there when the Dead Sea Scrolls were discovered.[30]

This suggestion makes sense since archaeologists found tens of thousands of fragments in Caves IVa and IVb. Perhaps full scrolls were removed from these caves in modernity or in medieval times. Flusser and Safrai's suggestion certainly also helps to explain why not one full scroll was recovered from "Cave IV" (as far as we now report). Those who found them, perhaps in the High Middle Ages, would have esteemed the works more than the more recent Bedouins who were looking for treasures like gold, coins, and precious artifacts; but even they eventually became aware of the value of smelly skins.

The observation by Flusser and Safrai that this psalm contains a word that appears only once in the Hebrew Bible but many times at Qumran and in our psalm in line 17b does not link it to Qumran; moreover, the text was read incorrectly (see the text and the note to 3.17). It is probable that our psalm antedates some Qumran compositions and was composed in Jerusalem, perhaps at the Temple, sometime before 100 BCE. It could not have been composed at Qumran because it contains a universalism that was anathema at Qumran and among the Essenes. (See the notes to the text and translation; esp. 2.8–12 and the expectation that "all worlds" will "know the LORD" in 3.16–18.) The universalistic perspective of MS RNL Antonin 798 clashes with the double

---

"The Prophet David at Qumran," 163.

30. Flusser and Safrai, "The Apocryphal Psalms of David," 266.

predestination of Qumran. As Bar-Ilan points out, the final lines could be recited by a non-Jew.[31]

More reflection indicates that the psalm was not composed at Qumran. The noun עולם means "world" and "age" in this psalm, but in the Qumran compositions it means almost always "eternity." Qumran scribes tended to avoid inscribing the *Tetragrammaton*; but in MS RNL Antonin 798 as in the Hebrew Bible, the *Tetragrammaton* is repeatedly presented in square script. That is anathema in Qumran compositions. In them we even find the *tetrapuncta* for the divine ineffable name (but the medieval scribe may have altered the text to the familiar square script). Thus, our psalm is not a Qumran composition, although it probably—along with many other compositions—was placed within the so-called Qumran Library. On target, yet vitiating much of what they had said, is Flusser and Safrai's last sentence: "We may conclude, then, that even though the Genizah Psalms demonstrate a marked affinity to the world of the Essenes, the portrait they sketch of the prophet David, along with their universal tone, accords with the environment that produced *Biblical Antiquities*."[32]

In light of the new edition and an examination of the text,[33] the most likely scenario is that this psalm was composed somewhere in ancient Palestine and taken to Qumran, being eventually placed in a cave. The celebration of the Temple, the adoration of the Davidic Psalter (the Hymnbook of the Second Temple), and the doxology, "Amen" to be said by the people of God indicate a cultic setting. The most appropriate one is the cult in the Jerusalem Temple. I have thus concluded that MS RNL Antonin 798 was composed in or near the Temple.

We may now focus on our fifth question: What name should be given to this psalm? Specialists in Second Temple Judaism should contemplate if the psalm in MS RNL Antonin 798 should be renamed "Psalm 156." Here are some reasons for this suggestion:

---

31. Bar-Ilan, "Non-Canonical Psalms from the Genizah," 700.
32. Flusser and Safrai, "The Apocryphal Psalms of David," 282.
33. See Charlesworth et al., "Appendix: Psalm 156."

Has Psalm 156 Been Found?

1. It is not authored by "David"; it is a David Pseudepigraphon composed in honor of David, and some passages are composed "out of the mouth of David,"[34] as in pseudepigraphical Psalms 151–155.[35]

2. The order and content of the psalms in the Davidic Psalter was not standardized before 70 CE, and many so-called apocryphal psalms were included; some psalters, for example, the pre-70 Qumran *Psalms Scroll*, contained "More Psalms of David."

3. We have early (pre-70) traditions that state David composed more psalms than are in the Davidic Psalter.

4. This psalm was most likely composed before 70 CE and in Hebrew.

5. It not only mentions "David" but attributes words and visions to him.

6. The psalm begins, or continues, on the top right of column 1; hence, any *incipit* would be lost. Experts might concur that this psalm should have a supernumerary for the following reasons:

   - In the judgment of most experts, the psalm was composed before the order and wording "150" psalms obtained a

---

34. Fleischer and Bar-Ilan deny that Psalm 156 is a pseudepigraphon of David, but a pseudepigraphon may be allegedly a composition by a biblical hero or attributed to him (as *1 Enoch* quotes Enoch in the third person). Psalm 156 does have first-person discourse, and the speaker seems to be David. As in many apocryphal texts, the transition between first-person discourse and third-person discourse is intermixed. Contrast Bar-Ilan, "Non-Canonical Psalms from the Genizah," 704.

35. Bar-Ilan wrongly accused Flusser and Safrai of concluding that the composition is a pseudepigraphon of David. Pseudepigraphical attribution was complex in Early Judaism and included many forms from first-personal speech to third-person speech; moreover, Deuteronomy is in third-person discourse but the *Temple Scroll* moves it to first-person discourse; thus, the text purports to present God's direct address to Israel.

norm and also before the Psalter was defined, closed, and canonized.[36]

- In 11QPs[a], the Hebrew copies of Psalm 151 A and 151 B (11Q5 28.3–14) have no numbers but are attributed to "David" in the title. Also in 11QPs[a], the title and first two lines of 154 are lost, and 155 has no title.

- In the Septuagint, Psalm 151 has no number, but it boasts this heading: "This psalm, though supernumerary, (is) David's own composition, when he single-handedly fought Goliath."

- In the Syriac manuscripts of the Peshiṭta, the title of Psalm 151 (A and B are one) is without number, deemed supernumerary, attributed to David, and considered David's own composition. In 152 and 153, the Syriac has only a title, attributing it to David. Psalms 154 and 155 have no number and a title that is very late; these last two psalms are attributed to Hezekiah.

Without specifications from the scribes of the manuscripts, scholars created and attached the numbers 151 A, 151 B, 152, 153, 154, and 155 to the psalms not found in the Masoretic Text. Since that text type is only one of the many text types in pre-70 Judaism, and since scholars added titles and numbers to these psalms, it seems prudent to add "Psalm 156" to another ancient psalm attributed to David. Otherwise it will be lost from discussions. Surely, to refer to it according to its catalogue number in a medieval Genizah misrepresents the composition and darkens counsel.

In light of the insights shared by the scholars who have devoted research to the psalm preserved in Saint Petersburg, I offer a hypothesis to test; it has the following six phases in the life of this Psalm of David.

---

36. See the recent massive study by Lee Martin McDonald, *The Formation of the Biblical Canon*, 229–31.

Has Psalm 156 Been Found?

Phase Six: Saint Petersburg. The manuscript is now placed in the National Library in Saint Petersburg (at that time, Leningrad).[37]

Phase Five: The Russian Archimandrite.[38] Archimandrite Antonin (1817–1894), the leading diplomat of the Russian mission in the Holy Land from 1865 to 1894, was a collector of manuscripts. He purchased this psalm when the manuscripts sequestered in the Cairo Genizah were sold.[39]

Phase Four: The Genizah. The ancient manuscript (now lost) was copied (perhaps more than once) and placed eventually in the Genizah of the Ezra Synagogue in Fostat (Old Cairo). Along with the *Damascus Document*, the *Aramaic Testament of Levi*, and other manuscripts, Psalm 156 would have been especially cherished by the Karaites in Cairo because they rejected the Rabbinic inclusion of the Oral Tradition and found God's Word only in the Hebrew Bible, notably for us in the Davidic Psalms.[40] The Karaites ("Scripturalists"), who appeared in the eighth century CE, called themselves *Bnai Mikra*, or "Sons of Scripture." A prominent leader was Anan ben David (flourished from 750 to 770 CE),[41] ostensibly of Davidic descent, who condemned the Talmudim and claimed each Jew had the right to interpret Torah. Since the Karaites were anti-Rabbinic, revered the pre-70 Sadducees, conceivably owed a significant debt to Qumran, and were focused on the Hebrew Bible

---

37. Katsh, *The Antonin Genizah*. Some of this information is now misleading. The sign B no longer applies, and the city is renamed.

38. Carmel, "Russian Activity in Palestine in the Nineteenth Century," 45–77. I am grateful to Meir Bar-Ilan for this bibliographical note. For Russian and European interest in "the Holy Land" in the nineteenth century, see Goren, et al., *Mapping the Holy Land*.

39. In Saint Petersburg, the Antonin Collection preserves approximately 1200 Hebrew manuscripts. The director of the Antonin Collection informed me that the vast majority of Antonin's manuscripts derive from the Cairo Genizah. See also Bar-Ilan, "Non-Canonical Psalms from the Genizah," 693.

40. See the succinct discussion in Stegemann, *The Library of Qumran*, 69–71. Also see Kahle, *The Cairo Geniza*, 16–17.

41. In or about 770 CE, Anan wrote *Sefer ha-mitzwot* or "The Book of Precepts." In it the TANAKH was the sole authority and was interpreted with freedom and also literalism. While Anan was a Persian, his followers lived primarily in Jerusalem and were known in Cairo.

(the TANAKH), including the Davidic Psalms, they would have admired and been stimulated by this psalm and others like it that they assumed were composed by David.[42] They would have felt elevated by a Psalm of David unknown to Rabbis. Anon ben David lived about the time this psalm was discovered near Jericho and when the Karaite Synagogue in Jerusalem commenced sometime in the eighth century CE. This Karaite Synagogue, in the Jewish Quarter of the Old City, is hailed as the "oldest synagogue" in Jerusalem and has been magnificently restored during the past decade.

Phase Three: Davidic Psalms found near Jericho. Origen (185–254 CE) in the third century CE[43] heard about the discovery of manuscripts near Jericho or Qumran. However, in his *Hexapla*, Origen comments only on Psalms 1–150.[44]

Timotheus I, the Nestorian Patriarch of Seleucia (= Baghdad), about 800 CE,[45] also knew about the discovery of previously unknown Davidic psalms. Through Timotheus's letter, we seem to learn that over two hundred Davidic Psalms were recovered by many Jews who went to retrieve the manuscripts. Here is the report from Otto Eissfeldt according to Millar Burrows:

> He [Eissfeldt] compared the discovery of the manuscripts [in the Qumran caves] with an earlier incident in the same region, related in a Syriac letter written about 800 A.D. by Timotheus, the Nestorian patriarch of Seleucia, to Sergius, the Metropolitan of Elam. Among other matters, Timotheus told Sergius of information he had

---

42. Astren, *Karaite Judaism and Historical Understanding*; Erder, "When Did the Karaites"; Erder, *The Karaite Mourners*; Wieder, *The Judean Scrolls and Karaism*. For a recent assessment of the Karities' indebtedness to Qumran, see Reif, "The Genizah and the Dead Sea Scrolls," esp. pp. 689–92.

43. Origen reported the discovery of a Greek version of the Psalter along with other Greek and Hebrew manuscripts in a jar near Jericho during the reign of Caracalla, who was emperor from 198 to 217 CE. See Mercati, ἔκδοσις εὑρθεῖσα μετὰ καὶ ἄλλων βιβλίων ἑβραϊκῶν καὶ ἑλληνικῶν ἔν τινι πίθῳ περὶ τὴν Ἱεριχὼ (*Letteratura Biblica e Cristiana Antica*, 29). The colophon continues to report that the cave was discovered during the reign of "Antoninos, the son of Severus" (188–217 CE), who is Caracalla.

44. See Field, ed., *Origenis Hexaplorum*, 305.

45. Braun, "Ein Brief des Katholikos Timotheos," 300–313.

HAS PSALM 156 BEEN FOUND?

received from some trustworthy Jews who had been instructed in the Christian faith. They said that books had been found ten years earlier in a cave near Jericho. An Arab hunter, whose dog had pursued an animal into the cave, followed it and found in the cave a little building containing many books. He informed the Jews of Jerusalem, who came in great numbers and found the books of the Old Testament and others in Hebrew writing, including more than two hundred psalms of David.[46]

We may assume that Jews took these Hebrew manuscripts, containing "more than 200 psalms of David," to Jerusalem, and the Karaites became fond of this "revelation" and support of the TANAKH. Scholars accurately surmise that the manuscript under discussion was one of these psalms. Obviously, although we will probably never know that our psalm was one of the two hundred, we must be open to the assumption that Psalm 156 was one of them, and that it was taken to Cairo and eventually placed in the Rabbinate Synagogue Genizah, which was founded in 882. This psalm had probably been transferred from the Karaite Synagogue nearby. Earlier, one can surmise, it had been in the ancient Karaite synagogue in Jerusalem.

Phase Two: At Qumran. About one thousand years earlier, the psalm was taken to Qumran, probably from Jerusalem, as is the case with many other scrolls found in the eleven Qumran caves. It would follow that this psalm was known to those in the Qumran Community before 68 CE.

Phase One: Jerusalem. The lost ancient manuscript (the *Urtext*), now represented by MS RNL Antonin 798, even earlier was composed in Jerusalem, most likely in the Temple (or nearby vicinity), probably sometime before 100 BCE.

Parts of this hypothesis are certain; others can never be proved or disproved. It is imperative to imagine and not discard such hypotheses. We have to trace the history of this manuscript

---

46. Otto Eissfeldt is the one who drew attention to Timotheus's letter to Sergius in the *Theologische Literaturzeitung*. Millar Burrows and J. T. Milik stimulated our thoughts about Timotheus I. The quotation is from Burrows, *The Dead Sea Scrolls*, 41. See also Milik, *Ten Years of Discovery*, 19.

before it was copied by a medieval scribe and then relegated to the Cairo Genizah.

Conclusion

At the outset, we indicated five issues in the *status quaestionis*. First, how many psalms are preserved in the medieval manuscript? Second, what is the date of this Psalm? Third, is this psalm "Davidic"? Fourth, what is the relation of this psalm to Qumran? Fifth, should this psalm be known as "Psalm 156"?

The following have been observed and should be in central focus in scholars' debates:

1. The major difference between my work and the scholarship of all others who have worked on this psalm is the perception that the manuscript may preserve one long psalm. It does not seem to be a prescription for psalms to be uttered on successive days of a month as in 4Q503. In contrast, Bar-Ilan concluded as follows: "In the heading of three liturgies, the date when the text should be recited is mentioned, as it is in Ps 91."

2. The work antedates 70 CE and may have been composed before 100 BCE. The original language is Hebrew, and the provenience is clearly ancient Palestine.

3. The psalm mentions "David," and the visions are most likely attributed to David.

4. The work is not similar to Qumran thought, and there are few parallels to the *Thanksgiving Hymns* (in contrast to the many hymns and psalms in the PTSDSSP 8B). The psalm was most likely composed in the Temple and taken to Qumran.

5. This psalm is like Psalms 151–155 and should be known as "Psalm 156."

4

The Importance of Psalm 156 for the Hebrew Bible, Early Judaism, and Christianity

In the preceding chapters we have disclosed that a virtually unknown leather manuscript in the National Library in Saint Petersburg, Russia, is ancient. Scholars tend to concur that it has an arresting history that covers about a thousand years. It is a lost psalm that is now found in its original language, Hebrew.

Studying the evolution of this manuscript and the learned publications of experts, I have discerned that the exciting psalm was probably composed in Jerusalem, and perhaps in the Temple before 100 BCE. It reflects the joy of the successes of the early Maccabees and Hasmoneans. The manuscript derives ultimately and evolves directly from the original Hebrew manuscript.

Eventually, probably a copy of the original was placed before 68 CE in a cave near Khirbet Qumran. Like the pre–70 CE compositions labeled the *Damascus Document* and the *Aramaic Testament of Levi*, it was taken to Cairo about 800 CE and eventually placed in a Rabbinate Genizah in the Ezra Synagogue in Fostat (Old Cairo) that was constructed about 882.

All who have only a cursory knowledge of the compilation of the Davidic Psalter know it evolved over many centuries. Many of the psalms in this Psalter are not attributed to David; yet Jesus and most of his contemporaries presupposed that all poetic compositions in the Davidic Psalter were composed by David.

Readers of the psalms, prayers, and odes in the *Old Testament Pseudepigrapha* know about Psalms 151–155. While the Masoretic Hebrew Bible and the Protestant Bible contain only 150 Davidic Psalms, Psalms 151–155 are preserved in ancient collections. To find all of them, scholars have to examine the Septuagint, the Qumran Corpus, and the early Syriac Psalter.

Some of the psalms in the "Davidic Psalter," as we have seen, are attributed to Solomon or another person. Psalms 154 and 155 (in Syriac) are attributed to Hezekiah while the Hebrew of Psalm 155 (11QPs^a 155) begins without attribution or number. We cannot discern any attribution in Psalm 156. The beginning of the psalm is now lost, but David is heralded in it as God's servant, and he has visions and speaks.

After editing the psalm in focus and Psalms 151–155, I have concluded that it should be recognized as a lost Psalm of David and known by the name *Psalm 156*.[1] I have no doubts it is pseudepigraphical and not a psalm composed by David. Based on my edition in the Princeton Dead Sea Scrolls Project, I wish now to focus on the importance of this Psalm for the Hebrew Bible, Early Judaism (300 BCE to 200 CE), and especially for Christian Origins.

The Importance of Psalm 156 for the Hebrew Bible

No barrier separates the early compositions in the Hebrew Bible, their expansions from the time of Solomon to the time of Ezra, and the literary creations of Early Judaism. The continuity of Isaiah (its expansion and interpolation from the eighth century BCE to about 300 BCE)[2] and especially the evolution of the Davidic

---

1. For additional observations that lead to this conclusion, see Charlesworth, "Is MS RNL Antonin 798 'Psalm 156'? This lecture was presented during the 2017 SBL International Meeting in Berlin. It is in preparation for publication.

2. See esp. the contributions in Charlesworth, ed., *The Unperceived Continuity of Isaiah*.

The Importance of Psalm 156

Psalter enriched the mind of the author of Psalm 156. The notes to my text and especially the translation of Psalm 156 point out the many echoes and quotations from the Hebrew Bible. In 1.23 the author of our psalm records an echo from Ps 89:28. Flusser and Safrai insightfully stated that Psalm 89 "exerted a great deal of influence on the description of David in our text."[3] Most importantly, in 2.24, the poet has echoed the well-known words in Ps 84:1–2,

> How lovely is your dwelling place,
> O Lord of hosts!
> My soul longs, indeed it faints
> For the courts of the Lord;
> my heart and my flesh sing for joy
> To the living God. [NRSV]

Other important quotations are in columns 3 and 4; note the following:

3.2 quotes Ps 105:2 (which appears without alteration in 1 Chr 16:9):

> O, chant to him; O, play a melody to him.
> Ponder all[4] his wonders.

4.8 quotes Ps 9:13 (probably from the Hebrew text represented by the LXX):

> He did not forget the cry of the afflicted

4.15 quotes Ps 106:48:

> Blessed be the Lord, the God of Israel
> From eternity to eternity
> Let all the people say, "Amen."

In addition, the author of Psalm 156 is indebted especially to the following passages in the Hebrew Scriptures (Old Testament): Pss

---

3. Flusser and Safrai, "The Apocryphal Psalms of David," 276.
4. An otiose *bet* is placed in Ps 105:2b and in 1 Chr 16:9.

24:1, 27:4, 40:4, 80:13[12], 106:24, 118:22, 120:5; and Isa 2:18, 20; 5:5; 21:1; 49:6; 52:10. Note the extreme importance of the Davidic Psalter and Isaiah.

There are parallels between Psalm 156 and other psalms attributed to David. The concept of living before God is found in the Psalter and in Psalm 156. The psalmist exclaims: "One (request) have I desired of the LORD: That I may dwell in the House of the LORD all the days of my life" (אַחַת שָׁאַלְתִּי מֵאֵת־יְהוָה אוֹתָהּ אֲבַקֵּשׁ שִׁבְתִּי בְּבֵית־יְהוָה כָּל־יְמֵי חַיַּי; Ps 27:4), and the composer of Psalm 156 reiterates this idea: "On account of you, thus, I wish (something) from you, / And this (is) my desire above all my requests: That I may live before you constantly" (בעבורך אני כן אשאל מפניך וזה חפצי על כל בקשותי כי אחיה לפניך תמיד; 3.1–2).[5]

Although the popular term for "psalm" (תהלה) does not appear in the manuscript, the following nouns are present: הודאה, זמיר, שיר, שירה, and תודה.[6] The manuscript clearly is a psalm in imitation of the Davidic Psalter, and we have now come to recognize that Psalm 156 is another psalm of David.[7] While only 1.15 explicitly mentions "David," who is the son of Jesse (1.15), there are multiple references to David throughout this psalm, and there are connections to other Davidic psalms. Psalm 151 parallels Psalm 156 by the mention of David being anointed (ומשחת [Ps 156 1.15], וימשחני [Ps 151 A 11, 11Q5 28.11], καὶ ἔχρισέν με [Ps 151 A 4c, LXX], ܘܡܫܚܢܝ [Ps 151 A 4c, Peshiṭta]).

This psalm contains a vision by an unnamed person, although David is named earlier. It is probable that David is the person who has the vision. According to Eupolemus, David had a vision when he wanted to build the Temple: "Since David wanted to build a temple for God, he asked God to show him a place for the altar. Then an angel appeared to him. . . ."[8] Eupolemus names

---

5 Note the use of שאל and בקש, as well as the parallel מֵאֵת־יְהוָה and מפניך.

6. I am indebted here to Stec, *The Genizah Psalms*, 5–6.

7. The author of 11Q5 reported that the total number of psalms and songs written by David was 4,050 with psalms alone numbering 3,600. (See 11Q5 27.5; see the text and translation in Charlesworth et al., eds., *Pseudepigraphic and Non-Masoretic Psalms and Prayers*.)

8 30:5, translated in Fallon, "Eupolemus."

The Importance of Psalm 156

the angel "Dianathan," which is clearly a combination of the Greek διά ("through") with the name "Nathan," the prophet who had the vision in the biblical account in 2 Sam 7. It is noteworthy that Eupolemus makes this shift to represent David as the visionary. As will become certain, there is additional evidence in other Early Jewish texts that suggests David was remembered to have been a visionary.

Pseudo-Philo implicitly mentions David's visionary ability in the exorcism song which David composed for Saul. It was *in nocte*, "in/by night," the time most associated with visions, that David went and sang the following to Saul:

> Darkness and silence (*tenebre et silentium*) were before the world was made, and silence spoke a word (*et locutum est silentium*) and the darkness became light. Then your name was pronounced in the drawing together of what had been spread out, the upper of which was called heaven and the lower was called earth. And the upper part was commanded to bring down rain according to its season, and the lower part was commanded to produce food for all things that had been made. And after these was the tribe of your spirits made. And now do not be troublesome as one created on the second day. But if not, remember Tartarus where you walk. Or is it not enough for you to hear that, through what resounds before you, I sing to many? Or do you not remember that you were created from a resounding echo in the chaos? But let the new womb from which I was born rebuke you, from which after a time one born from my loins will rule over you.[9]

The *Pesharim* include commentaries on the Davidic Psalms (4Q171, 1Q16, 4Q173); thus, the Qumranites, and other early Jews, most likely believed that David had prophetic powers.

Prophecy is also associated with David in 2 Samuel. The psalm contained in 2 Sam 23:1–7 is called an "oracle of David" (נְאֻם דָּוִד). Then David speaks: "The spirit of the LORD speaks through me, his word is upon my tongue. The God of Israel has

---

9. *Ps-Philo* 60:2–3, translated in Harrington, "Pseudo-Philo."

spoken, the Rock of Israel has said to me ..." (2 Sam 23:2–3). This quotation is the closest biblical passage in which David seems to be like a prophet, but while the passage contains a prophetic oracle, no word for "prophet" is present. The author of Acts reports that David was a prophet (Acts 2:30). David is additionally portrayed as a prophet in later documents, especially *b. Sotah* 48b and the *Targum on the Psalms* (18:1, 49:17, 103:1).

David's Compositions in 11Q5 speaks of the marvelous accomplishments and characteristics of David, but it does not mention that he was a visionary. He was "wise" (חכם), "a light" (ואור), "literate" (וסופר), "discerning" (ונבון), and "perfect" (ותמים). God "gave him a discerning and enlightened spirit" (רוח נבונה ואורה); he wrote thousands of psalms and songs which "he composed through prophecy" (דבר בנבואה).[10] Psalm 156, however, is the first extant record of David's visions.

The Importance of Psalm 156 for Early Jewish Thought and Early Judaism

This psalm adds to our knowledge of early Jewish thought. God is known as "the God of Israel." God is not presented according to Qumran's preference. The Qumranites understood God as "the God of knowledge." The perception is known from the *Rule of the Community* (esp. 1QS 3).

The month "Iyyar" does not appear in the Hebrew Bible. It is the Babylonian name of the month; most likely this name began to be used during and after the Babylonian Captivity. The month is mentioned at the beginning of each vision. According to 1 Kgs 6:1, Solomon began to build the Temple, "the House of the LORD," in "the second month," called "Ziv" (= Iyyar), which means "glow" or "blossom" in Hebrew (and derives from Akkadian (*zīm/wu* and *ayyaru*). It is the month in which Shavuot is celebrated and the second month in the Jewish liturgical calendar; today it begins in April or May, according to the Gregorian Calendar. "Iyyar" (אייר

---

10. See 11Q5 27.2–11.

The Importance of Psalm 156

or (איר) is somehow related to "light" (אור) and during the Hasmonean period, when Psalm 156 was probably composed, the *yodh* (אייר or איר) and *waw* (אור) are often indistinguishable for paleographers today.

Research should be focused on why the author chose Iyyar for the visions (cf. *m. Rosh Ha-Shanah* 3). In Rabbinics or medieval Jewish imagination, each day of Iyyar had significance. Is Psalm 156 the first evidence of this interpretation? Iyyar much later came to be an acronym for the Hebrew "I, YHWH who heals you" (כִּי אֲנִי יְהוָה רֹפְאֶךָ; Exod 15:26). Did early Jews believe that "manna" first appeared in Iyyar, and if so does that help us comprehend why a Jew would choose Iyyar as the month for David's visions?

The text is not rabbinic; Rabbis almost always chose יי (the abbreviation YY) and not יהוה (YHWH not to be pronounced) for the *Tetragrammaton*. The *Tetragrammaton* in Psalm 156 may be presented as it was imagined in the time of David, and not as it was at Qumran and in other groups or sects in Early Judaism; perhaps this is a result of pseudepigraphical authorship and the honoring of David.[11]

The poet ponders theodicy. In 1.2 he states that God is the "Judge ... in righteousness." Later in 4.18–19, he adds that God is the "Judge of righteousness," and "a false judgment shall not go out from before you." Thus, whatever happens on earth and to humans is the result of God's righteous judgment. Bar-Ilan rightly discerns that this poet weaves his "theology into liturgical verses"; indeed, such rhetoric is "a unique feature of this text."[12]

Sharing the thought of many early Jews, the author of Psalm 156 portrays God as "the judge of generations and the one ruling in righteousness." God is the Creator, who "divided the world

---

11. See Flusser and Safrai, "The Apocryphal Psalms of David," 264: "Moreover, he writes all this in the style of the psalms, which leads us to the conclusion that this is the remnant of pseudepigraphal psalms attributed to David himself. Confirmation that this view comes from the author's desire to be associated with a biblical character is evident in his decision to write out the tetragrammaton, a decision dutifully followed by the copyist of the Genizah manuscript, who apparently recognized the special nature of the text."

12. Bar-Ilan, "Non-Canonical Psalms from the Genizah," 701.

between darkness and light" (1.2). God is the God of all Israel; he is not the God of knowledge of the *Rule of the Community* (1QS 3).

Psalm 156 adds to our resources for early Jewish obsession with God in the Holy Land before 70 CE. Despite the Greek, Roman, and Parthian invasions, God is the cosmic Judge and Creator (1.1–4), who continues to be involved in history and directing the faithful to better times. God has purified and renewed the nation (1.5–12) and forgiven "all our sins" (1.13–14). Such a confession harmonizes with the annual confessions of sin and reception of atonement on the *Day of Atonement* (Yom Kippur; see Lev 16:19–20), especially in the Temple cult.

Adoration of King David is in the mind of the author of Psalm 156. God pledged to David, who is God's servant, and anointed him "the Shoot of Jesse" so that "righteousness and justice" were multiplied in his days" (1.15–20). David is "an eternal column," and he broke through the wall and "the splendor of all the Gentiles" (1.17 and 19d). In the future, God will support David. He will be greater than "all the angels" forever (1.21–27). The author lauded David but he did not claim David, or anyone, to be "the Anointed One" or "the Messiah."

Some Jews who lived at a time after the composition of this psalm may have used such concepts and terms and imagined David was portrayed as "the Anointed One," "the Messiah." But, clear references to a Messiah who is cosmic, will change the world, and usher in the final days (the eschaton) appear with lucid clarity only later. They can be found in the *Rule of the Community* (1QS) and most importantly in the *Psalms of Solomon*. As is well known, these compositions took shape much later than Psalm 156, perhaps fifty years later and in the first century BCE. The generic "messianic" innuendoes about David help to date Psalm 156 sometime in the second century BCE.

For clarification of the adulation, but not necessarily messianic portrayal, of David, note particularly 1.15–20 (italics added for emphasis):

> You made a pledge ahead to *David your servant*,
> And *you anointed* with compassion *the Shoot of Jesse*.

You sustained his arm through your holiness,
For he established your praise unto the ends of the earth.

(As) *an eternal pillar* you set his name;
And he is breaking through the wall and rebuilding the ruins.

(David is) *a cornerstone* despised which the builders despised,
And you raised (him) to be *head above all the nations*.

Magnificence and a crown you have allowed him to inherit with rejoicing,
And the splendor of all the Gentiles you are calling his name.

Righteousness and justice you multiplied in his (David's) days;
And peace and blessings forever without number.

The optimistic tone of this Palestinian Jew probably antedates the Roman incursion of 63 BCE. Following that date, according to Josephus, "we lost our freedom and became subject to the Romans" (*Ant.* 14.77).

The three visions attributed to David (2.5–12, 3.10–21, and 4.16–23) all occur in the month of Iyyar; perhaps the Psalm contained readings for certain days in the Temple. Thanksgivings, rejoicings, and blessings characterize the optimistic tone (2.13–16, 2.20–27, 3.6–9). Idol worship has ended (2.17–19), reflecting the success of the Maccabees. Signaled out for celebration is the Lord's graciousness (4.1–7) and his incomparable mercies (4.8–12).

Psalm 156 increases our knowledge of beatitudes in Palestinian Judaism from 300 BCE to 132 CE (the beginning of the Bar Kokhba Revolt). Jewish beatitudes appear in Sirach (14:20–27, 25:8–9, 26:1), 4 Maccabees (7:15), 1QH^a (6.13–15), 4Q185 (frgs. 1–2 2.8, 13–14), 4Q525 (the Qumran Beatitudes), 1QM (13.2), Matthew (5:1–12; 11:6; 13:16; 16:17; 24:46), Luke (1:45; 7:23; 10:23; 11:27, 28; 12:37, 38, 43; 14:14, 15; 23:29; 6:20–23), John (13:17; 20:29), Romans (4:7, 8; 14:22), James (1:12; 1:25), Revelation (1:3; 14:13; 16:15; 19:9; 20:6; 22:7, 14), *History of the Rechabites* (14:5);

Has Psalm 156 Been Found?

Gospel of Thomas (54; 68–69a; 69b), and *2 Enoch* (58:2; 42:6–14; 52:1–15). The beatitudes in Psalm 156 are in 1.27, 3.1, and 4.24, 26:

> Fully joyful is the one who finds glory in the desires of your will ... (3.1)
> Fully joyful is the one purified by your holiness ... (4.24)
> Fully joyful are those who keep your commands. (4.26)[13]

As the above excerpts prove, Psalm 156 offers beatitudes that are inclusive of all humans; they are not focused on males. In contrast to the focus on "man" (הָאִישׁ) in Ps 1:1 and a beatitude in Psalm 156 at 1.27 in which we find a beatitude focused on "the man" (הגבר), the majority of beatitudes in Psalm 156 (3.1, 4.24, 26), as in *4QBeatitudes* (4Q525), *2 Enoch*, Matthew, and Luke, are generic and inclusive.

Psalm 156, like *4QBeatitudes* and *2 Enoch*, proves that Jesus's symbolic thought was shaped by many types of Judaism. Those to whom he was closest no longer were constrictive and dominated by males who considered women inferior. Jesus's inclusion of women was not acceptable to the Sadducees and many priests, scribes, and even some Pharisees. Psalm 156 thus adds to our knowledge of the esteem of women in Early Judaism, placarded by the expansive narratives in the *Testament of Job, Pseudo-Philo, Joseph and Aseneth*, the egalitarian seating in pre-70 synagogues, and the archives of Babatha.[14]

In this manner, Psalm 156 adds to the evidence of universalism (see the notes to my translation of Psalm 156 in PTSDSSP 9A) and beatitudes that encompass all humanity. In my translation, the concept of "Adam" has been restored to its original meaning, representing both male and female, since אדם means "human." Additionally, David's kingship is expressed in universalistic ways. Notice this excerpt that also elevates David and portrays him as "king of all the nations":

---

13. I have chosen "fully joyful" and not "blessed" to represent these beatitudes, as it better represents the original Hebrew; "blessed" is reserved for ברוך.

14. For the most recent publication, see Esler, *Babatha's Orchard*.

> Above all the angels you made his greatness;
> And king of all the nations you placed him for eternity. (1.23)

Many passages preserve the traditional celebration of Israel, but note 2.8–12, which express hope for the nations and their inclusion in the time to come:

> Because for the good of the world you have allowed me to stand before you.
> And for a light (to) the Gentiles you commissioned me with your strength.
>
> All the nations will recount your glory.
> For they will see your righteousness through the hand of your faithful ones.
>
> Let them gather: The officials and all the kings of the earth,
> The princes of the inhabited-world, the rulers of the human,
>
> So they may see the mighty (deeds) of your right hand,
> And to discern the mystery of your holy words.
>
> Then all of them will comprehend your might.
> For your hand, O LORD, has been doing all these things

Obviously, an interpretation of Isaiah, notably Isaiah 42–46 (Second Isaiah), echoes in these lines.

Psalm 156 thus adds to the evidence of universalism and beatitudes that encompass all humanity. The concept of "Adam" has been restored to its original meaning, representing both male and female and all humanity. Our increased knowledge of beatitudes in Early Judaism from Psalm 156 helps us understand Jesus's teachings in their original setting.

The Importance of Psalm 156 for Christian Origins

Psalm 156 increases the perception that many phrases, concepts, and metaphors found in the documents collected into the New

Testament are not only adumbrated but articulated in early Jewish thought. Here are nine selected examples for further research on Psalm 156 and Christian Origins.

First, as demonstrated in the previous section, Psalm 156 preserves previously unknown beatitudes in 3.1, 4.24, and 4.26. Jewish beatitudes appear in many documents, including documents in the Hebrew Scriptures, Apocrypha, Pseudepigrapha, and New Testament; at Qumran; and from Rabbinics (see Appendix 1). Jesus is famous for his use of beatitudes, found especially in Matthew and Luke, but more attention should be in focus on Jesus's relation with the continuity of Jewish beatitudes.

Second, as expounded upon earlier, Psalm 156 offers beatitudes inclusive of all humans; they are not focused on males. The majority of beatitudes in Psalm 156 (3.1, 4.24, 26), as in *4QBeatitudes* (4Q525), *2 Enoch*, Matthew, and Luke, are generic and inclusive. Jesus's thought was related to the type of Judaism that was shaking off the mantel of patriarchalism. Note the well-known opening of Matthew's "Sermon on the Mount" (cf. Luke 6:20–26):

> When Jesus saw the crowds, he went up the mountain; and after he sat down, his disciples came to him. Then he began to speak, and taught them, saying:
>
> "Fully joyful are the poor in spirit, for theirs is the kingdom of heaven.
>
> "Fully joyful are those who mourn, for they will be comforted.
>
> "Fully joyful are the meek, for they will inherit the earth.
>
> "Fully joyful are those who hunger and thirst for righteousness, for they will be filled.
>
> "Fully joyful are the merciful, for they will receive mercy.
>
> "Fully joyful are the pure in heart, for they will see God.
>
> "Fully joyful are the peacemakers, for they will be called children of God.
>
> "Fully joyful are those who are persecuted for righteousness' sake, for theirs is the kingdom of heaven.

The Importance of Psalm 156

> "Fully joyful are you when people revile you and persecute you and utter all kinds of evil against you falsely on my account. Rejoice and be glad, for your reward is great in heaven, for in the same way they persecuted the prophets who were before you. (Matt 5:1–12; NRSV)[15]

Third, our increased knowledge of beatitudes in Early Judaism helps us understand Jesus' teachings in their original setting. The universalism and eschatological hope found in Psalm 156 help us understand Paul's arresting claim that all Israel will be saved (Rom 11:26), which is an echo from Isaiah 59 (which according to some scholars is Third Isaiah).

Fourth, scientific research and *prima facie* evidence indicate that Jesus frequently imagined he had a prophetic and messianic self-understanding; that is the case with the person in focus in our psalm. Abraham A. Harkavy (1835–1919) stated in 1902 that the psalm preserves "the prayers and praises of a man who apparently thought of himself as a prophetic and messianic figure."[16] I am convinced that these thoughts are not claims by the author of the psalm; they are attributed to David. We should distinguish clearly between the imaginations of the author and the author's celebration of David. He alone receives two visions and is anointed. We should hesitate to categorize Psalm 156 as a messianic text. The New Testament preserves evidence that Jesus had a prophetic and a messianic self-understanding. Only one example must suffice; it is Mathew's redaction of Mark 8:29–30, 33. In Matt 16:16–17, Jesus accepts Peter's claim the he is the Messiah:

> Simon Peter answered and said: "You are the Christ, the Son of the living God." Jesus answered and said to him, "Blessed are you, Simon Bar-Jonah, for flesh and blood has not revealed (this) to you, but my Father who is in heaven. (NSRV)

---

15. To harmonize with the translation of the beatitudes in Psalm 156, I have changed "Blessed are" to "Fully joyful are."
16. Harkavy, *Ha-Goren*, 82–85.

Has Psalm 156 Been Found?

If Peter had made this confession in Hebrew, it would be: "you are the Messiah, the Son of the living God" (אתא המשיח בן אלהים חיים).

Fifth, the celebration of David in Psalm 156 was composed during the period of the evolution of messianic ideology. It is possible to interpret 1.15–20 as messianic, but the term "Messiah" does not appear. Clearly, some Jews later probably read it as messianic, and David, "the Shoot of Jesse" is "anointed" (1.15). Since, according to Jewish lore and teaching, only God can declare who is the Messiah, Jesus probably did not proclaim that he was "the Messiah." Redaction, and later elements in the Gospels, provide that claim, and Jesus's early followers made that proclamation central to their claims. Many Jews who claimed Jesus was the Messiah, and had been with Jesus or seen him in Galilee or Judea, referred to him as "Jesus the Christ." Some of the earliest evidence may be in Paul's life before he composed his epistles.

Sixth, as mentioned earlier, David is hailed to be greater than the angels: "*Above all the angels* you made his greatness" (1.23 [italics added]). Hence, David is greater than Uriel, Michael, and other archangels. These terms and a similar claim reappear in reference to Jesus in many New Testament passages and in Peter's confession that Jesus is "like a righteous angel" (*ekeine Nouaggelos Ndikaios*), according to the *Gospel of Thomas* 13. Does the qualifying and delimiting adjective "righteous" indicate knowledge of the evil angels (perhaps in Genesis 6 and *1 Enoch*)?

As is well known, the author of Hebrews claimed that God's Son is greater than the angels: τοσούτῳ κρείττων γενόμενος τῶν ἀγγέλων (Heb 1:4). Jesus's status is higher than any of the angels. Psalm 156 provides evidence that some Jews, much earlier, had used similar concepts for David. Thus, Psalm 156 adds to the insights we obtain from other challenging compositions, namely the *Self-Glorification Hymn* and *11QMelchizedek*.

Seventh, the author of Psalm 156 celebrates God's Kingdom and frequently conflates it with David's kingdom. In interpreting the psalm, I have often been impressed that God's Kingdom and David's kingdom are not distinguished. The two references

The Importance of Psalm 156

to David's kingdom are 3.15 and 4.4. David, not God, was given "daughters of Jerusalem for the beauty of his kingdom," and God is the one who "appointed his servant, / (with) splendor, and majesty, and the glory of his kingdom." But in 4.9 God's Kingdom is in focus: "I remembered the strengths and the might of his kingdom and the beauty of his might." The words are attributed to David: "Blessed be the glorious name of his kingdom forever and ever" (4.14). Hence, often the author employs "his," and the reference could be to God or to David, the two dominant figures in this psalm. Some early Jews would imagine that the "kingdom" promised to David should be perceived in light of the Kingdom of God.

This conflation and identification helps us understand the context and meaning of Jesus's fundamental teaching: The dawning of the Kingdom of God. Specialists in Jesus research have shown that Jesus drew on many traditions when he proclaimed the dawning of God's Kingdom, including the eschatological visions of apocalyptic Judaism, the Son of Man as Judge found in the *Parables of Enoch*,[17] and the Davidic kingdom repeatedly celebrated in Hebrew Scriptures and the apocryphal compositions. The Evangelists proclaimed the connection between David's kingdom and Jesus's kingdom. Notice this famous passage presented as poetry (italics added for clarity):

> He (Jesus) will be great, and be called *the Son of the Most High*;
> And the Lord God shall give unto him the throne of his father *David*.
> And he shall reign over *the house of Jacob* for ever;
> And of *his kingdom* there shall be no end. (Luke 1:32–33; NRSV)

The traditions preserved in Psalm 156 add fresh insights into Jesus's world and mind. In light of the adoration of David in Psalm 156, we may better understand why Jesus stressed that as God supported David and established his kingdom, now God is also

---

17. See my suggestion that Jesus was influenced by those who were composing the *Parables of Enoch*. See Charlesworth and Bock, eds., *Parables of Enoch*.

Has Psalm 156 Been Found?

inaugurating an eschatological Kingdom. Jesus was convinced that God was now saving his people as promised by the prophets.

Eighth, the disciples (as well as Paul) who crafted the early proclamations (*kerygmata*) celebrated Jesus's most prominent disciples as "pillars" (Gal 2:9; cf. 1 Tim 3:15; Rev 3:12, 10:1). This symbolism echoes not only 1 Kgs 7:21 and perhaps Prov 10:25 but also, unperceived until now, our psalm, in which David is called "an eternal pillar" (1.17).

Ninth, the passage that deserves intensive exploration in light of Psalm 156 is Heb 1:4. According to this verse, Jesus's status is higher than any of the angels; and according to 1:5-6 the "angels worship him" (= the Son). We have sufficient evidence that Adam, Abel, Enoch, Noah, Abraham, Melchizedek, Jacob, Moses, Levi, Elijah, the anonymous one in the *Self-Glorification Hymn*, and others were considered angelomorphic humans by some early Jews—that is, these biblical luminaries were superhuman and more like the angels.[18] We also know that the Qumranites imagined that the most perfect of the Holy Ones transmographied from a human (ἄνθρωπος) to an angel (ἄγγελος).[19] We should now comprehend that the perspective of Ps 156 1.23 and Heb 1:4 is uniquely parallel. Do the parallels not suggest some relation between these two compositions? That relation is heightened by terms shared in Heb 1:1-4 with Psalm 156; noteworthy are "these last days" and "the glory of God." Emphasized in Hebrews, in contrast to Psalm 156, is the claim that the Son "created the world" and "bears the very stamp of his nature" (1:2-3). It is certain that the author of Hebrews was a learned Jew who became a Christian; did he know Psalm 156?

The author of Ps 156 1.18 applies Ps 118:22 to David, but this attribution is not chosen by the author of Hebrews, although it is attributed to Jesus in Mark 12:10, Matt 21:42, and Luke 20:17

---

18. See Gieschen, *Angelomorphic Christology*. Gieschen demonstrates that "angelomorphic traditions played a significant role in early Christology, including the Christology found on the pages of the NT" (p. 349). Now, we need to add the insights obtained by studying Psalm 156.

19. Charlesworth, "The Portrayal of the Righteous as an Angel," 135-51.

and cited as proof of Jesus's messiahship in a speech attributed to Peter (Acts 4:11), in 1 Pet 2:7, and in the *Gos. Thom.* 66. Recall Ps 118:22, "The stone (that) the builders rejected, / Has become the chief cornerstone." Perhaps some of Jesus's followers knew what we learned recently from archaeology: Golgotha is a rejected quarry stone because of the cracked rock.[20]

The traditions in Psalm 156 enrich our exegesis of Hebrews and entice us to ponder how and in what ways these Jewish traditions shaped the origins of Christianity. The difference is between ideology and Christology. Pointing to the Hebrews author's elevation of the Christ above Moses (3:2-6) and Abraham (since Christ is like Melchizedek; 7:4-10), Flusser and Safrai rightly claimed that "the midrashic tradition that elevates the Messiah above Abraham, Moses, and the angels antecedes the Epistle to the Hebrews."[21]

Thus, Psalm 156 foreshadows a considerable amount of the symbolic language once thought to be creations of Jesus's followers. It also offers topoi used by many New Testament authors. Again, we find how Jewish are Jesus, those in the Palestinian Jesus Movement, and almost all the authors of New Testament works. Marc Philonenko and Alfred Marx rightly judged Psalm 156 to be "of exceptional importance for the history of speculations focused on David in Early Judaism."[22]

Conclusion

The discovery of Psalm 156 and research upon this virtually unknown psalm enriches our evaluation of early Jewish writers and thinkers and the emergence of what will be categorized as "Christian." We now have a clearer perception of the adoration of David which goes far beyond his portrayal in Chronicles, the Apocrypha, and the Pseudepigrapha. With this psalm, we have a better

---

20. See my discussion of Ps 118:22 in Charlesworth, *Jesus within Judaism*, 124-25.

21. Flusser and Safrai, "The Apocryphal Psalms of David," 273.

22. Philonenko and Marx, "Quatre 'Chants' Pseudo-Davidiques trouvés dans la gueniza du Caire et d'origine Esséno-Qoumrânienne," 390.

appreciation of the memory and hope of the early Jews as they crafted a visionary and prophetic understanding of David. Early Jewish creations show oppressions due to repeated subjugations to foreign powers; they also, and more importantly, reveal a resilience that affirmed an optimism for God's continuing involvement with Israel, God's beloved people. Pondering Psalm 156 and the context it mirrors, we see more traditions that most likely had fundamental importance for the minds of Jesus and his followers.

Conclusion

This monograph introduces a document virtually unknown to many experts, including those specializing in Early Judaism. The composition does not appear in any collection of ancient psalms, odes, or prayers. It is not mentioned in introductions or erudite studies on the Davidic Psalms, nor is it included in the study of the hymns, odes, psalms, and prayers found among the over one thousand Qumran Manuscripts.

An image, transcription, translation, and introductory explorations are provided in this monograph. The leather manuscript of the psalm under scrutiny is preserved now in the National Library in Saint Petersburg, Russia. It is MS RNL Antonin 798 and clearly made its way there from Jerusalem in modernity.

What has been examined is a medieval scroll that was once part of the Cairo Genizah. It was probably taken to Fostat (Old Cairo) and placed in the Ezra Synagogue and later moved to the Rabbinate Genizah. The psalm should be recognized, in light of Psalms 151–155, as "Psalm 156." Translations and discussions of Psalms 151 A, 151 B, 152, 153, 154, and 155 are included before a detailed study of the psalm in MS RNL Antonin 798. All of these psalms are preserved in Syriac and are part of the Syriac Bible, the Peshitta.

Why has "Psalm 156" not been included in the Peshitta? No one can be certain what facts or observations help us answer this new question. Most likely, copies of it, and of other now lost psalms, were destroyed when Jerusalem was burned from 66 to

70 CE. Conceivably, the only surviving copy of "Psalm 156" was hidden in a Judean cave, most likely one of the caves near Qumran.

The manuscript is not a medieval composition and was not composed by the Essenes. Like *Words of the Lights* (4Q504–506; 4QDib Ham^{a-c}), Psalm 156 is free of Qumran *termini technici* and emphases which shape the *Prayers for Festivals* (1Q34, 1Q34^{bis}; 4Q507–9). As suggested in the previous pages, most likely Psalm 156 was found before 800 CE in a cave near Jericho or Qumran. Arguments are presented why this psalm was composed probably in Jerusalem, perhaps in the Temple, sometime before 100 BCE.

Psalm 156 is long and is almost as extensive as Psalm 119. David is mentioned in this psalm, and he is given revelatory visions. These are not previously found in the pre-70 Jewish compositions. The valuable document helps us comprehend the genius of the early Jews, many of whom, like the Righteous Teacher, Hillel, and Jesus, were obsessed by spirituality and God, the creating Creator. The composition helps us better appreciate the indebtedness of "Christianity" to early Jewish literature and thought.

Appendix 1: On Beatitudes

We know about the composition of beatitudes in many countries. We also know that the love of beatitudes antedates Early Judaism (300 BCE to 200 CE). Beatitudes are found in early Egypt, the classical world, biblical texts, the Dead Sea Scrolls, the Apocrypha, the Pseudepigrapha, the New Testament, the Apocryphal New Testament, inscriptions, and Rabbinics. In Hebrew, the focus should be on אשרי, "fully joyful is," which is translated by and fundamentally synonymous with the Greek μακάριος. Appreciably different is ברוך, "blessed is," which is equal to εὐλογητός and is usually reserved for God.[1] Here is my list of the most important beatitudes; in the Hebrew Bible and Qumran Scrolls. They are usually introduced by אשרי:

Ramses II [1200 BCE? Cf. Cazelles, *TDOT* 1.483]

Petosiris [c. 150 BCE?]

Homer, *Odyssey* 5, 7 and 24, 191–92 [the beatitude is addressed to God]

Petronius, *Satyricon* 94,1 [blessing of a mother]

Hesiod [*TDNT* 4.365]

Gen 30:13 [the naming of Asher]

Deut 33:29 ["Blessed are you, O Israel"]

Ps 1:1

---

1. See Ps 28:6, 31:22, etc. Note esp. the use of ברוך with God or the Lord in Ps 103:1, 2, 20, 21, 22 [*bis*].

Appendix 1

Ps 32:1–2

Ps 33:12 ["Blessed is the nation whose God is the LORD"]

Ps 40:5

Ps 41:2 [41:14 is ברוך]

Ps 65:5

Ps 84:5, 6

Ps 89:16

Ps 94:12

Ps 106:3

Ps 112:1

Ps 119:1, 2

Ps 128:1

Ps 156 1.27, 3.1, and 4.24, 26

Prov 29:18

Prov 28:14

1 En 58:2 ["Blessed are you, O righteous and elect ones"]

2 En 42:6–14 [9 beatitudes in both (J) and (A)]

2 En 52:1–15 [7 beatitudes and 6 curses in both (J) and (A)]

Sir 14:20–27

Sir 25:8–9 [3 beatitudes]

Sir 26:1

4 Macc 7:15 ["O blessed old age . . . life loyal to the Torah"]

1QH^a 6.13–15 [restored]

4Q185 frgs. 1–2 2.8, 13–14 [in a wisdom context]

4Q525 [in a composition devoted to wisdom; 4 beatitudes with a part of another]

1QM 13:2 ["Blessed be the God of Israel . . . Bl[es]sed be they . . ."]

Appendix 1: On Beatitudes

Matt 5:1–12 [9 beatitudes]

Matt 11:6; 13:16; 16:17; 24:46

Luke 1:45; 7:23; 10:23; 11:27, 28; 12:37, 38, 43; 14:14, 15; 23:29

Luke 6:20–23 [4 beatitudes plus 4 woes]

John 13:17; 20:29

Rom 4:7, 8; 14:22

Jas 1:12; cf. 1:25

Rev 1:3; 14:13; 16:15; 19:9; 20:6; 22:7, 14

HistRech 14:5 ["Blessed (are) you . . ."][2]

Gos. Thom. 54 ["Blessed are the poor"]

Gos. Thom. 68–69a [blessed are "you" (then, "they" who are persecuted)]

Gos. Thom. 69b [blessed are the hungry]

ActsPaul 5–6

Jewish tombstone [c. 4–6 cent. CE; CIJ 2.1175]

b. Berakot 61b ["Blessed are you, Rabbi Akiba"]

b. Hagîgâ 14b [a blessing by ben Zakkai to two of his disciples]

b. Homa 86a

It becomes clear that a vast majority of the biblical beatitudes appear in the Davidic Psalter and collections in *2 Enoch*, Sirach, 4Q525, Matthew, and Luke. In Early Judaism the beatitudes appear in Wisdom literature, apocalyptic literature, and hymnic compositions; the literary forms use second- and third-person discourse. Studying the beatitudes in *2 Enoch*, Sirach, and 4Q525, we comprehend that the collection of beatitudes is not unique to Matthew and may go back to Jesus; the beatitudes are not necessarily Matthew's redactional additions. Moreover, while Qumran frames the beatitudes with Wisdom Traditions, Matthew 5 and Luke 6 (and most likely Jesus) present them with an eschatological emphasis.

---

2. The text concerns "the Blessed Ones." For the Greek, see Charlesworth, ed. and trans., *The History of the Rechabites*; the quotation is from p. 79.

Appendix 2

Images and Transcription
MS RNL Antonin 798
Antonin Collection, St. Petersburg[1]

---

1. We are pleased to publish these images of MS RNL Antonin 798. They were provided to us courtesy of the Russian National Library. James H. Charlesworth well remembers the gracious way he was received at the Russian National Library in Saint Petersburg.

Appendix 2

Column 1

בלו לפניך צדיק ורשע
דיין רוחות ושופט בצדק
חפצת בצדק ומאסת בעול
והבדלתה עולם ביומ חושך לאור
ודיתה מעמד כלבב זרים
חוכמת עוד נתתה לעבדך
טעתה צדקות בארץ אמת
ילמדו שיר כל עובדי שמך
כנגד כל הארץ ירבו צדיקתם
כונות דרכם אל מעוזך
לעולם לעולם יעבדו את שמך
מי כמעשיך וכי כפועליך
מחלת וסלחת את כל חטואתינו
נבאת ברחוק על פי עבדך
נשבעתה מראש לדויד עבדך
סמכת וידיעו בזדו ושתנך
עמוד עולם שמיתה את שמו
פנה כי נואסה אשר מאסו הבונים
פאר ועטרת הינחלתו בריינה
צדיק ומשפט הרביתה בימיו
עהדלו לפניך כל בחורי צדק
קרשת על פי את עום הגדול
רוב כל מלאכים עשית גדולתו
שברית לפמו כל מלכי מרים
תמכת ימיני על חרבי וחמצתי זה רע
לא ימיטו רגלי כי בטוח בשענך
אשרי הגבר אשר בטח בידך

ולא תבקיש שלחם עניו דאס
יודע כרימו כל רוי
ולא יתיצבו חוללים לנגד מביטיך
וכיז טמא לטהור ובין צדיק לש...
וטוהרית צאנך מן חיה טומאה
כי ניבון בכולם מחפצי רצונך
ומשפטו הרביתה בעולמות
אשר ראיונו כדברי עבדיך
ופועלי טומעה אשר אהב כלכמס
ויותר עד מחוג מצד נעשי פלאך
רוצא נציחים יודעמו את שומך
ותפיר ירמהו יד על רב כל מעשיך
תפארת באחד על כל פשעינו
כי אישע קצו ערד לא תאחיר
ומשחת באחוםך אין עורייעו ושרי
כי הזמן שבועך יעד אפסני ארץ
ונדיר פרץ ומנה בורך...
ועליון לראשמיעל מן אומים
והוד כל הגוים קיאת את אמעך
ושלום וברכת ...
כי ישמחו עול...
ושירוך על ...
ומכל כל האורים נושי בצאה
ותבעת במצולות כל שונאי נפשך
על כל גבורי קדר
ולא יכשל כוח עבוריך מאתתיך
... ובלימו פיגו ...

1	גלוי לפניך צדיק ורשע	ולא תבקיש עליהם עידי אדם
2	דיין דורות ושופט בצדק	יודיע בדרכי כל חי
3	חפצת בצדק ומאסת בעוול	ולא יתיצבו הוללים לנגד כבודך
4	והבדלתה עולם בין חושך לאור	ובין טמא לטהור ובין צדק לשקר
5	זריתה מעמך כל בני זרים	וטהרת צאנך מן חיה טמאה
6	חוכמת עוזך נתתה לעבדך	כי מיבין בכולם בחפצי רצונך
7	טעתה צדקות בארץ אמת	ומשפט הרביתה בעולמים
8	ילמדו שיר כל עובדי שמך	אשר יאמינו בדבריך עבדך
9	כנגד כל הארץ ירבו צדקתם	ופועלי טובתם אשר אהבו בלבבם
10	כוננת דרכם אל מצותיך	וישרת כוחם בכל מעשי פלאך
11	לעולם לעולם יעבדו את שמך	ולנצח נצחים ירוממו את שמך
12	מי כמעשיך ומי כפועליך	ומי ידמה לך על רב כל מעשיך
13	מחלת וסלחת את כל חטאתינו	וכפרת באהבה על כל פשעינו
14	ניבאת ברוחך על פי עבדך	כי קרבתי קץ ועוד לא תאחר
15	נשבעת מראש לדויד עבדך	ומשחת ברחמך את שורש ישי
16	סמכת זרועו בקדושתך	כי היכין שבחך עד אפסי ארץ
17	עמוד עולם שמתה את שמו	וגודר פרץ ובונה חורבות
18	פינה ממואסה אשר מאסו הבונים	ועלית לראש מעל כל האומים
19	פאר ועטרת הינחלתו ברינה	והוד כל הגוים קראת את שמו
20	צדק ומשפט הרבית בימיו	ושלום וברכות עד בלי מספר
21	צהלו לפניך כל בחירי צדק	כי ישמחו בארץ חמדה
22	קדשת על פיו את שם הגדול	ושירות עוזך יספר כל יום
23	רוב כל מלאכים עשית גדולתו	ומלך כול האומים נתתי לנצח
24	שברת לפניו כל מלכי מדין	וטבעת במצולות כל שונאי נפשו
25	תמכת ימינו על חרבו וחזקת זרועו	על כל גבורי קידר
26	לא ימוט רגלו כי בטח בשמך	ולא יכשל כוחו כי עזרתו באהבה
27	אשרי הגבר אשר יבטח בדברך	כי לעולם לעולם לא נכלמו פניו

Appendix 2

Column 2

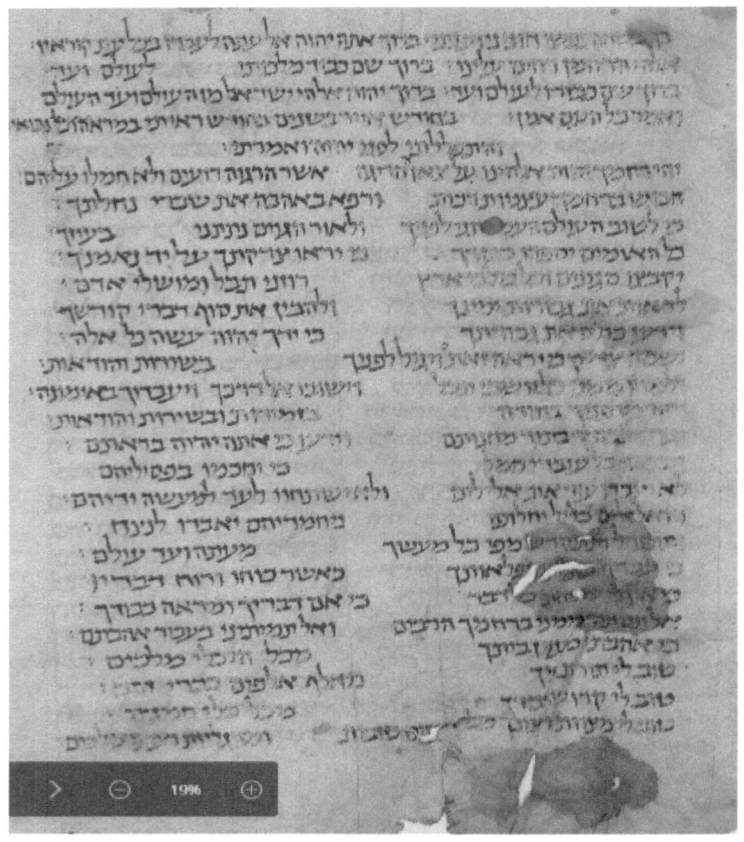

1	בך בטחה נפשי חוניני ועניני ברוך אתה יהוה אל עונה לעבדו בכל עת קוראיו
2	אלהי הרחמן רחים עלינו ברוך שם כבוד מלכותו לעולם ועד
3	ברוך שם כבודו לעולם ועד ברוך יהוה אלהי ישראל מן העולם ועד העולם
4	ואמר כל העם אמן: בחודש אייר בשנים בחודש ראיתי במראה וכל נבואיו והתפללתי לפני יהוה ואמרתי
5	יהי רחמך יהוה אלהינו על צאן ההריגה אשר הרגו הרועים ולא חמלו עליהם
6	חבוש ברחמך עצמות רכות ורפא באהבה את שברי נחלתך
7	כי לטוב העולם העמדתני לפני ולאור הגוים נתתני בעוזך
8	כל האומים יספרו כבודך כי יראו צדקתך על יד נאמנך
9	יקבצו סגונים וכל מלכי ארץ רוזני תבל ומושלי אדם
10	לראות את גבורות ימינך ולהבין את סוף דברי קודשך
11	וידעו כולם את גבורתך כי ידך יהוה עשה כל אלה
12	ישמח צדיק כי יראה זאת ויגיל לפניך בשירות והודאות
13	ילמדו ממני כל יושבי תבל וישובו אל דרכך ויעבדוך באימונה
14	ויקדמו פניך בתודה בזמירות ובשירות והודאות
15	יגדלו כבודך בתוך מחנותם וידעו כי אתה יהוה בראתם
16	ויבושו כל עובדי סמל כי יחכמו בפסליהם
17	לא יעבדו עוד את אלילים ולא ישתחוו לעד למעשי ידיהם
18	והאלילים כליל יחלופו מחמדיהם יאבדו לנצח
19	ותתגדל ותתקדש מפי כל מעשיך מעתה ועד עולם
20	כי עבדך יספר בנפלאותך כאשר כוחו ורוח דבריו
21	כי אין לו שמחת כל דבר כי אם דבריך ומראה כבודך
22	אל תסתיר ממני ברחמך הרבים ואל תמיתיני בעבור אהבתם
23	כי אהבתי מעון ביתך מכל היכלי מלכים
24	טוב לי תורת פיך מאלף אלפים ככרי זהב
25	טוב לי קדוש דברך מכל כלי חמדה
26	טוב לי מצוות רצונך מכל אבנים טובות ומרגליות חפצי מלכים

Appendix 2

Column 3

1 אשרי שימצא כבוד בחפצי רצונך   ובעבורך אני כן אשאל מפניך
2 וזה חפצי על כל בקשותי   כי אחיה לפניך תמיד
3 ואהליך בצדקתך בלא עון ואדריף   באמיתך כל יום כאשר יושר בעיניך
4 אל תמנע ממני את שאלתי ועשה בקשתי כחפצי רצונך
5 אעמוד בהם עד עולם   לדעת כל נתיבי צדקך
6 ברוך אל עושה זאת   ברוך פועל את כל אלה
7 ברוך אשר בחר בעבדו   וימלא אותי כל משאלות לבי
8 ברוך שם כבוד מלכותו לעולם   ברוך שם כבודו לעולם ועד
9 ברוך יהוה אלהי ישראל מן העולם ועד העולם   ואמר כל העם אמן:
10 בשלשה בחדש אייר ראיתי במראה וכל נבואיו והתפללתי לפני יהוה ואמרתי
11 ברוך מוריש ומעשיר   ומבורך משפיל ומרים
12 כי הקים מעפר דל   ומאשפות הירים אביון
13 ויגדל כסאו מעל כל השרים   ויגביר כוחו על כל מושלים
14 ויתן לו כל חמדת מלכים   וחיל גוים ואוצרות מלכים
15 בנות מלכים לכבודו   ובנות ירושלם לתפארת מלכותו
16 אשריו יאמרו כל העולמים   ולפניו ישתחוו כל תקומי הארץ
17 ויבטחו ביהוה כי הגדיל לעשות   ולא יטעו עוד בהבל ומשם
18 כי כולם ידעו את יהוה   מגדולי אדם ועד קטני אינוש
19 כי יהוה שופט בכל העולם   אחד משפיל ואחד מירים
20 לאשר ירצה יתן   ולאביוני אדם ירש נחלה
21 כי בידו נפש כל חי   ורוח כל בשר אליו ישתחוו
22 שירו לו זמרו לו   שיחו כל נפלאותיו
23 שירו לשמו בכל עת   כי לו נאה תפארת ועוז
24 אשר היציל מצרה את נפש אוהביו   ומיד כל מרעים רוח חסידיו
25 כי בטח בשמו ובכבוד מראה   ובדברי קודשו ובכל דרכי חיים
26 לעד נעבוד את שמו   ולנצח נצחים נגיד גבורתו

Appendix 2
Column 4

1 כי הוא רופא לנשברי לב	וחובא את עצם דכים
2 והוא הפך דויה לשמחה	וזיע ורתית למבטחות גדולות
3 כי לו ארץ ומלאה	תבל וכל יושבי בה
4 כי מלפניו צוה על עבדו	הוד והדר וכבוד מלכותו
5 אשר חפץ בטוב עמו	ושלח הרופא ורפא בשרם
6 והכביד תורתו על פי עבדו	ומצות דברו על ידי נאמנו
7 הירבה בלבו חוכמה ובינה	ורב קדושתו עד בלי מספר
8 מי דומה לו ומי כמותו	אשר לא שכח צעקת אביון
9 וזכר ברחמיו עני ודל וגם אנכי כי זכרתי	גבורות ועוז ממשלתו ותפארת עזו
10 לילה ויום אעמוד לפניו	ואברך את זכרו על כל מעשיו
11 תתברך ותתרומם אדון כל הדורות תתקדש ותתפאר מושיל בכל מעשיו
12 תתיחד מלכי מפי כל משרתך	שופט צדק ודיין אמת
13 ברוך אתה יהוה אל נא זוכר ברחמיו	את ברית עבדו לנצח
14 ברוך שם כבוד מלכותו לעולם ועד ברוך שם כבודו	לעולם ועד
15 ברוך יהוה אלהי ישראל מן העולם ועד העולם ואמר כל העם אמן:
16 בארבעה בחודש אייר ראיתי ברוח במראה הקודש וכל נבואיו
והתפללתי לפני יהוה ואמרתי
17 ברוך כי שבר רשעים	והעמיד קרן צדיקים
18 ודעתו וחכמתו בכל לבי	כי אתה הוא שופט הצדק
19 ולא יצא מלפניך משפט שקר	כי אם אמת ואמונה
20 תתן לאדם כדרכיו	וכפרי מעלליו תשיב לו
21 אין כחש בכל מעשיך	ואין כזב בכל דבריך
22 כל פועלך תמים יחד	ועול בל ימצא במעשך
23 כנהר שוטף הירביתה משפטך	וכזרע מבורך הצמחתה צדקתך
24 אשרי יזכה בקדושתך	יספר כבודך בכל יום
25 עזרתי מלפני כבודך	לאוכל לנצח לעמוד ברצונך
26 כי ת[ם]היום	אשרי שומרי פקודיך

Bibliography

Astren, Fred. *Karaite Judaism and Historical Understanding*. Studies in Comparative Religion. Columbia: University of South Carolina Press, 2004.
Auffret, Pierre. "Structure littéraire et interpretation du Psaume 155 de la grotte XI de Qumrân." *RQ* 9 (1978) 323–56.
Baars, Willem. "Apocryphal Psalms." In *The Old Testament in Syriac, according to the Peshitta Version*, vol. 4, fas. 6, edited on behalf of the International Organization for the Study of the Old Testament by the Peshiṭta Institute of the University of Leiden, vol. 4, fas. 6, pp. i–x Vetus Testamentum Syriace iuxta simplicem Syrorum versionem. Leiden: Brill, 1972.
Bar-Ilan, Meir. "Non-Canonical Psalms from the Genizah." In *The Dead Sea Scrolls in Context: Integrating the Dead Sea Scrolls in the Study of Ancient Texts, Languages, and Cultures*, edited by Armin Lange et al., 2:693–718. 2 vols. VTSup 140/2. Leiden: Brill, 2011.
Braun, Oscar. "Ein Brief des Katholikos Timotheos I über biblische Studien des 9. Jarhhunderts." *Oriens Christianus* 1 (1901) 300–313.
Burrows, Millar. *The Dead Sea Scrolls*. New York: Viking, 1955.
Carmel, Alex. "Russian Activity in Palestine in the Nineteenth Century." In *Vision and Conflict in the Holy Land*, edited by Richard I. Cohen, 45–77. Jerusalem: Yad Ben-Zvi, 1985.
Carmignac, Jean. "Nouvelles Precisions sur le Psaume 151." *RQ* 8 (1975) 593–97.
Charlesworth, James H. "Ashkar Manuscript 2: Introducing a Phenomenal New Witness to the Bible." *Israel Museum Studies in Archaeology* 7 (2015) 66–69.
———. "The Concept of the Messiah in the Pseudepigrapha." In *Aufstieg und Niedergang der römischen Welt: Geschichte und Kultur Roms sim Spiegel der neueren Forschung*, Band II.19,1, edited by Wolfgang Haase, 188–218. Berlin: de Gruyter, 1979.
———. "From Jewish Messianology to Christian Christology: Some Caveats and Perspectives." In *Judaisms and Their Messiahs at the Turn of the*

Christian Era, edited by Jacob Neusner et al., 225–64. Cambridge: Cambridge University Press, 1987.

———. *Jesus within Judaism*. ABRL. New York: Doubleday, 1988.

———. *The Pesharim and Qumran History: Chaos or Consensus?* With appendixes by Lidija Novakovic. Grand Rapids: Eerdmans, 2002.

———. "The Portrayal of the Righteous as an Angel." In *Ideal Figures in Ancient Judaism: Profiles and Paradigms*, edited by John J. Collins and George W. E. Nickelsburg, 135–51. SBLSCS 12. Chico, CA: Scholars, 1980.

———, ed. and trans. *The History of the Rechabites*. SBLTT 17. Pseudepigraph Series 10. Chico, CA: Scholars, 1982.

———, ed. *The Unperceived Continuity of Isaiah*. Jewish and Christian Texts 28. London: Bloomsbury T. & T. Clark, 2018 [in press].

Charlesworth, James H., and Darrell L. Bock, eds. *Parables of Enoch: A Paradigm Shift*. Jewish and Christian Texts in Contexts and Related Studies 11. T. & T. Clark Library of Biblical Studies. London: Bloomsbury, 2013.

Charlesworth, James H., et al. "Appendix: Psalm 156." In PTSDSSP 9A, forthcoming.

———. "The Hodayot." In PTSDSSP 5A, forthcoming.

———. "Non-Masoretic Psalms." In *Pseudepigraphic and Non-Masoretic Psalms and Prayers*, edited by James H. Charlesworth et al., 155–215. PTSDSSP 4A. Tübingen: Mohr/Siebeck, 1997.

Charlesworth, James H., et al., eds. *The Messiah: Developments in Earliest Judaism and Christianity*. Minneapolis: Fortress, 1992.

———, eds. *The New Jerusalem and Related Literature*. PTSDSSP 8B. Tübingen: Mohr/Siebeck, forthcoming.

———, eds. *Qumran-Messianism: Studies on the Messianic Expectations in the Dead Sea Scrolls*. Tübingen: Mohr/Siebeck, 1998.

Charlesworth, James H., and James A. Sanders. "More Psalms of David." In *OTP* 2:609–24.

Cross, Frank Moore. "David, Orpheus, and Psalm 151:3–4." *BASOR* 231 (1978) 69–71.

———. "The History of the Biblical Text in Light of the Discoveries in the Judaean Desert." In *Qumran and the History of the Biblical Text*, edited by Frank Moore Cross and Shemaryahu Talmon, 177–95. Cambridge: Harvard University Press, 1975.

Dobbs-Allsopp, F. W. *On Biblical Poetry*. New York: Oxford University Press, 2015.

Dunn, James D. G. *Jesus and the Spirit: A Study of the Religious and Charismatic Experience of Jesus and the First Christians as Reflected in the New Testament*. NTL. Philadelphia; Westminster, 1975.

Eissfeldt, Otto. "Der gegenwärtige Stand der Erforschung der in Palästina neu gefundenen Hebräischen Handschriften." *TLZ* 74/10 (1949) 595–600.

Engel, Edna, and Mordechai Mishor. "An Ancient Scroll of the Book of Exodus: The Reunion of Two Separate Fragments." *Israel Museum Studies in Archaeology* 7 (2015) 24–60.

Erder, Yoram. *The Karaite Mourners of Zion and the Qumran Scrolls*. Tel Aviv: Hakibbutz Hameuchad, 2014.

———. "When Did the Karaites First Encounter Apocalyptic Literature Akin to the Dead Sea Scrolls?" *Cathedra* 42 (1987) 54–68 and 85–86.

Esler, Philip F. *Babatha's Orchard: The Yadin Papyri and an Ancient Jewish Family Tale Retold*. Oxford: Oxford University Press, 2017.

Evans, Craig A. "The Reputation of Jesus in Light of Qumran's Tradition of David as Prophet." In *Reading the Bible in Ancient Traditions and Modern Editions; Studies in Textual and Reception History in Memory of Peter W. Flint*, edited by Andrew B. Perrin et al., 629–51. SBLEJL 47. Atlanta: SBL Press, 2017.

Even-Shoshan, A. מִלּוֹן אֶבֶן־שׁוֹשָׁן (*Even-Shoshan Dictionary*). Tel Aviv: ha-Milon he-ḥadash, 2003.

Fallon, Francis T. "Eupolemus." In *OTP* 2:861–72.

Field, Frederick, ed. *Origenis Hexaplorum*. 2 vols. Hildesheim: Olms, 1964.

Fleischer, Ezra. "Medieval Hebrew Poems in Biblical Style." *Te'uda* 7 (1991) 200–248.

Flint, Peter W. *The Dead Sea Scrolls and the Book of Psalms*. STDJ 17. Leiden: Brill, 1997.

———. "The Prophet David at Qumran." In *Biblical Interpretation at Qumran*, edited by Matthias Henze, 158–67. Studies in the Dead Sea Scrolls and Related Literature. Grand Rapids: Eerdmans, 2005.

Flusser, David, with Shemuel Safrai. "The Apocryphal Psalms of David." In *Judaism of the Second Temple Period*. Vol. 1, *Qumran and Apocalypticism*, 258–82. Translated by Azzan Yadin. Grand Rapids: Eerdmans, 2007.

Gieschen, Charles A. *Angelomorphic Christology: Antecedents and Early Evidence*. ABAJU 42. Leiden: Brill, 1998.

Goren, Haim, et al. *Mapping the Holy Land: The Foundation of a Scientific Cartography of Palestine*. Tauris Historical Geography Series 11. London: Tauris, 2017.

Haran, Menahem. *The Biblical Collection: Its Consolidation to the End of the Second Temple Times and Changes of Form to the End of the Middle Ages*. 4 vols. Jerusalem: Bialik Institute, 1996.

Harkavy, A. E. "Prayers in the Style of the Songs of the Psalms by an Anonymous Person" (Heb.). *Ha-Goren: Abhandlungen über die Wissenschaft des Judenthums* 3 (1902) 82–85.

Harland, P. J. "בָּלַע I *bālaʿ*." In *TWQ* 1:458–59.

Harrington, Daniel J. "Pseudo-Philo." In *OTP* 2:298–377.

Hurtado, Larry W. *Lord Jesus Christ: Devotion to Jesus in Earliest Christianity*. Grand Rapids: Eerdmans, 2003.

———. *One God, One Lord: Early Christian Devotion and Ancient Jewish Monotheism*. Philadelphia: Fortress, 1988.

———. *One God, One Lord: Early Christian Devotion and Ancient Jewish Monotheism*. Cornerstones Series. London: Bloomsbury T. & T. Clark, 2015.

BIBLIOGRAPHY

Hurvitz, Avi. "Observations on the Language of the Third Apocryphal Psalm from Qumran." *RQ* 5 (1965) 225-32.

Jastrow, Marcus. *A Dictionary of the Targumim, the Talmud Babli and Yerushalmi, and the Midrashic Literature.* New York: Judaica, 1971.

Kahle, Paul E. *The Cairo Geniza.* 2nd ed. Oxford: Blackwell, 1959.

Katsh, Abraham Isaac. *The Antonin Genizah in the Saltykov-Schedrin Public Library in Leningrad.* New York: Institute of Hebrew Studies, New York University, 1963.

Knauf, Ernst Axel. "Kedar." In *ABD* 4:9-10.

———. "Μαδιάμα." *ZDMG* 135:16-21.

Kugel, James L. *The Idea of Biblical Poetry: Parallelism and Its History.* New Haven: Yale University Press, 1981.

Krarup, Ove Chr., ed. *Auswahl pseudo-Davidischer Psalmen: Arabisch und Deutsch.* Copenhagen: Gad, 1909.

Lee, Samuel. *Vetus Testamentum Syriace.* London: Impensis Ejusdem Societatis, 1823.

Loke, Andrew Ter Ern. *The Origin of Divine Christology.* SNTSMS 169. Cambridge: Cambridge University Press, 2017.

Lorein, G. W., and Eveline van Staalduine-Sulman. "A Song of David for Each Day: The Provenance of the Songs of David." *RQ* 85 (2005) 33-59.

———. "Songs of David: A New Translation and Introduction." In *Old Testament Pseudepigrapha: More Noncanonical Scriptures Volume 1*, edited by Richard Bauckham et al., 257-71. Grand Rapids: Eerdmans, 2013.

Lowth, Robert. *De sacra poesi hebræorum: Prælectiones academicæ oxonii habitae.* Edited by David A. Reibel. Robert Lowth (1710-1787): The Major Works. London: Routledge/Thoemmes, 1995.

———. *Isaiah: A New Translation.* Edited by David A. Reibel. Robert Lowth (1710-1787): The Major Works. London: Routledge/Thoemmes, 1995.

———. *Lectures on the Sacred Poetry of the Hebrews.* Edited by David A. Reibel. Robert Lowth (1710-1787): The Major Works. London: Routledge/Thoemmes, 1995.

———. *The Life of William of Wykeham, Bishop of Winchester.* Edited by David A. Reibel. Robert Lowth (1710-1787): The Major Works. London: Routledge/Thoemmes, 1995.

———. *The Major Works.* Edited by David A. Reibel. 8 vols. London: Routledge/Thoemmes, 1995.

———. *Sermons, and Other Remains of Robert Lowth.* Edited by David A. Reibel. Robert Lowth (1710-1787): The Major Works. London: Routledge/Thoemmes, 1995.

Magne, Jean. "Orphisme, pythagorisme, essénisme dans le texte hébreu du Psaume 151?" *RQ* 8 (1975) 508-47.

———. "Le Psaume 154." *RQ* 9 (1977) 95-102.

———. "Le Psaume 155." *RQ* 9 (1977) 103-11.

———. "Les Textes grec et syriaque du Psaume 151." *RQ* 8 (1975) 548-64.

McDonald, Lee Martin. *The Formation of the Biblical Canon*. 2 vols. 4th ed. London: Bloomsbury, 2017.

Mendenhall, George E. "Midian." In *ABD* 4:815–18.

Mercati, Giovanni. *Note di letteratura Biblica e Cristiana antica*. Studi e testi (Bibliogeca apostolica vaticana) 5. Rome: Tipograpfia Vaticana, 1901.

Milik, J. T. *Ten Years of Discovery in the Wilderness of Judaea*. Translated by John Strugnell. Studies in Biblical Theology 1/26. London: SCM, 1959.

Miller, Eric. "The Self-Glorification Hymn Reexamined." *Henoch* 31/2 (2009) 307–24.

Miller, Patrick D. *Interpreting the Psalms*. Philadelphia: Fortress, 1986.

Philonenko, Marc, and Alfred Marx. "Quatre 'Chants' Pseudo-Davidiques trouvés dans la gueniza du Caire et d'origine Esséno-Qoumrânienne." *Revue d'histoire et de philosophie Religieuses* 77 (1997) 385–406.

Pigué, Stanley C. "Psalms, Syriac (Apocryphal)." In *ABD* 5.536–37.

———. "The Syriac Apocryphal Psalms: Text, Texture, and Commentary." PhD diss., Southern Baptist Theological Seminary, 1988.

Polzin, Robert. "Notes on the Dating of the Non-Massoretic Psalms of 11QPsa." *HTR* 60/4 (1967) 468–76.

Pouilly, Jean. *La Règle de la Communauté de Qumrân: Son evolution littéraire*. Cahiers de la Revue Biblique 17. Paris: Gabalda, 1976.

Reibel, David A., ed. *Robert Lowth (1710–1787): The Major Works*. 8 vols. London: Routledge, 1995.

Reif, Stefan C. "The Genizah and the Dead Sea Scrolls." In *The Dead Sea Scrolls in Context: Integrating the Dead Sea Scrolls in the Study of Ancient Texts, Languages, and Cultures*, edited by Armin Lange et al., 2:689–92. 2 vols. VTSup 140/2. Leiden: Brill, 2011.

Sanders, James A., ed. *The Dead Sea Psalms Scroll*. Ithaca: Cornell University Press, 1967.

———. *The Psalms Scroll of Qumrân Cave 11 (11QPsa)*. DJD 4. Oxford: Clarendon, 1965.

Seow, C. L. *Myth, Drama, and the Politics of David's Dance*. HSM 44. Atlanta: Scholars, 1989.

Skehan, Patrick W. "A Broken Acrostic and Psalm 9." *CBQ* 27/1 (1965) 1–5.

———. "Qumran and Old Testament Criticism." In *Qumrân: Sa piété, sa théologie, et son milieu*, edited by M. Delcor, 163–82. BETL 46. Paris: Duculot, 1978.

Smith, Morton. "Two Ascended into Heaven: Jesus and the Author of 4Q491." In *Jesus and the Dead Sea Scrolls*, edited by James H. Charlesworth, 290–301. New York: Doubleday, 1992.

Stec, David M. *The Genizah Psalms: A Study of MS 798 of the Antonin Collection*. Cambridge Genizah Studies Series 5. Études sur le Judaïsme médiéval 57. Leiden: Brill, 2013.

Stegemann, Hartmut. *The Library of Qumran: On the Essenes, Qumran, John the Baptist, and Jesus*. Grand Rapids: Eerdmans, 1998.

Strugnell, John. "Notes on the Text and Transmission of the Apocryphal Psalms 151, 154 (= Syr. II) and 155 (= Syr. III)." *HTR* 59/3 (1966) 257–81.

Talmon, Shemaryahu. *The World of Qumran from Within: Collected Studies.* Leiden: Brill, 1989.

Toorn, Karel van der. "Celebrating the New Year with the Israelites: Three Extabiblical Psalms from Papyrus Amherst 63." *JBL* 136 (2017) 633–49.

Welch, John W., ed. *Chiasmus in Antiquity: Structures, Analyses, Exegesis.* 1981. Reprint, Provo, UT: Research Press, 1999.

Wernberg-Møller, Preben. "The Nature of the YAHAD according to the Manual of Discipline and Related Documents." *ALUOS* 6 (1966–1968) 56–81.

Westermann, Claus. *The Living Psalms.* Translated by J. R. Porter. Grand Rapids: Eerdmans, 1989.

———. *Praise and Lament in the Psalms.* Translated by Keith R. Crim and Richard N. Soulen. Richmond: John Knox, 1981.

———. *The Psalms: Structure, Content, and Message.* Translated by Ralph D. Gehrke. Minneapolis: Augsburg, 1980.

Wieder, Naphtali. *The Judean Scrolls and Karaism.* London: East and West Library, 1962.

Wilson, Gerald H. *The Editing of the Hebrew Psalter.* SBLDS 76. Chico, CA: Scholars, 1985.

Yardeni, Ada. *The Book of Hebrew Script: History, Palaeography, Script Styles, Calligraphy & Design.* Rev. and exp. from the original Hebrew ed. Jerusalem: Carta, 1997.

BIBLIOGRAPHY

Psalms 151-156: A Selected Bibliography by Brandon L. Allen

This bibliography lists all the major publications on Psalms 151-156. They are presented in the following order: Survey Studies, Psalms 151-155 Collectively, Psalm 151 A and B, Psalm 152, Psalm 153, Psalm 154, Psalm 155, Psalm 156, and Psalms 151-155 and Qumran Hymns and Prayers. These psalms were considered part of the Hebrew Bible by many Jews before 70 CE, or even possibly before 135/6 CE, and may have been considered canonical before the canon was closed. One is placed in the Septuagint, some in the Qumran *Psalms Scroll*, and many appear in the Peshiṭta.

Survey Studies

Charlesworth, James H. "Jewish Hymns, Odes, and Prayers (ca. 167 BCE—135 CE)." In *Early Judaism and Its Modern Interpreters*, edited by Robert A. Kraft and George W. E. Nickelsburg, 411-36. The Bible and Its Modern Interpreters 2. Atlanta: Scholars, 1986.

———. "Jewish Prayers in the Time of Jesus." *Princeton Seminary Bulletin* Supplement Series 2 (1992) 36-55.

———. "A Prolegomenon to a New Study of the Jewish Background of the Hymns and Prayers in the New Testament." In *Essays in Honour of Yigael Yadin*, edited by Jacob Neusner and Geza Vermes, 265-85. Journal of Jewish Studies 33. Oxford: Oxford Centre of Postgraduate Hebrew Studies, 1982.

Charlesworth, James H., with James A. Sanders. "More Psalms of David." In *OTP* 2:609-24.

Cohen, Shaye J. D. "The Temple and the Synagogue." In *The Early Roman Period*, edited by William Horbury et al., 298-325. Cambridge History of Judaism 3. Cambridge: Cambridge University Press, 1999.

Elbogen, Ismar. *Der jüdische Gottesdienst in seiner geschichtlichen Entwickllung*. Frankfurt: Kauffmann, 1931.

Flusser, David. "Psalms, Hymns and Prayers." In *Jewish Writings of the Second Temple Period*, edited by Michael E. Stone, 551-77. CRINT 2.2. Assen: Van Gorcum, 1984.

Heinemann, Joseph. *Prayer in the Talmud: Forms and Patterns*. SJ 9. Berlin: de Gruyter, 1977.

Hoffman, Lawrence. H. *The Canonization of the Synagogue Service*. University of Notre Dame Center for the Study of Judaism and Christianity in Antiquity 4. Notre Dame, IN: University of Notre Dame Press, 1979.

Hornig, Barbara. "Das Prosagebet der nachexilischen Zeit." PhD diss., Universität Leipzig, 1957.

Hurvitz, Avi. "Psalms, Apocryphal." In *EncyJud* 13.1302–3.
Jansen, Herman Ludin *Die spätjüdische Psalmendichtung: Ihr Entstehungskreis und ihr "Sitz im Leben." Eine literaturgeschichtliche-soziologische Untersuchung*. Skrifter utgitt av det Norske Videnskaps-Akademi i Oslo. Historisk-Filosofisk Klasse 3. Oslo: Dybwad, 1937.
James, M. R. "Apocrypha." In *Encyclopaedia Biblica* 1:249–61.
Johnson, Norman Burrows. *Prayer in the Apocrypha and Pseudepigrapha: A Study of the Jewish Concept of God*. JBLMS 2. Philadelphia: Society of Biblical Literature and Exegesis, 1948.
Lattke, Michael. *Hymnus: Materialien zu einer Geschichte der antiken Hymnologie*. NTOA 19. Freiburg, Switzerland: Universitätsverlag, 1991.
Manns, Frédéric. *La prière d'Israel à l'heure de Jésus*. Analecta (Studium Biblicum Franciscanum) 22. Jerusalem: Franciscan, 1986.
Mayer, Günter. "Die Funktion der Gebete in den alttestamentlichen Apokryphen." In *Theokratia: Jahrbuch des Institutum Judaicum Delitzschianum II (1970–1972). Festgabe für Karl Heinrich Rengstorf zum 70. Geburtstag*, edited by Wolfgang Dietrich et al., 16–25. Leiden: Brill, 1973.
Pigué, Stefan. C. "Psalms, Syriac (Apocryphal)." In *ABD* 5:536–37.
Rief, Stefan C. "The Early Liturgy of the Synagogue." The Early Roman Period, edited by William Horbury et al., 326–57. The Cambridge History of Judaism 3. Cambridge: Cambridge University Press, 1999.
Trafton, John L. "Psalms, Apocryphal." In *Mercer Dictionary of the Bible*, edited by Watson E. Mills et al., 722. Macon, GA: Mercer University Press, 1990.
Van Rooy, H. F. "The Psalms in Early Syriac Tradition." In *The Book of Psalms Composition and Reception*, edited by Patrick D. Miller and Peter W. Flint, 537–50. VTSup 99. Leiden: Brill, 2005.
Wanke, Gunther. "Prophecy and Psalms in the Persian Period." In Introduction, edited by William Horbury et al., 162–88. Cambridge History of Judaism 1. Cambridge: Cambridge University Press, 1999.
Westermann, Claus. "Psalmen, syrische." In *BHH*, edited by Bo Reicke and Leonhard Rost, 3:1522–23. 4 vols. Göttingen: Vandenhoeck & Ruprecht, 1960.
Zorn, Reinhard. "Die Fürbitte im Spätjudentum und im Neuen Testament." PhD diss., Universität Göttingen, 1957.

BIBLIOGRAPHY

Psalms 151–155 Collectively

Baars, Willem. "Apocryphal Psalms." In *The Old Testament in Syriac according to the Peshitta Version*, edited on behalf of the International Organization for the Study of the Old Testament by the Peshiṭta Institute of the University of Leiden, vol. 4, fas. 6, pp. i–x. Vetus Testamentum Syriace iuxta simplicem Syrorum versionem. Leiden: Brill, 1972.

Baumstark, Anton. *Geschichte der syrischen Literatur, mit Ausschluß der christlich-palästinensischen Texte*. Bonn: A. Marcus und E. Webers, 1922.

Brock, Sebastian P. "Jewish Traditions in Syriac Sources." *JJS* 30/2 (1979) 212–32.

Charlesworth, James H. "Syriac Psalms, Five Apocryphal (Five Psalms of David, Psalms 151–155)." In *The Pseudepigrapha and Modern Research with a Supplement*, 202–9. SBLSCS 7. Chico, CA: Scholars, 1981.

Charlesworth, James H., with James A. Sanders, "More Psalms of David." In *OTP* 2:609–24.

Delcor, M. "Cinq nouveaux psaumes esséniens?" *RQ* 1 (1958) 85–102.

———. *Les hymnes de Qumrân (Hodayot)*. Paris: Letouzey et Ané, 1962.

———. "Zum Psalter von Qumran." *BZ* 10 (1966) 15–29.

Fabricius, Johann Albert. *Codex Pseudepigraphus Veteris Testamenti*. Hamburg: Christiani Liebezeit, 1713.

Krarup, Ove Chr., ed. *Auswahl pseudo-Davidscher Psalmen, Arabisch und Deutsch*. Copenhagen: Gad, 1909.

Maier, Johann. *Die Qumran-Essener: Die Texte vom Totem Meer*. Vol. 1, *Die Texte der Höhlen 1–3 und 5–11*. Uni-Taschenbücher 1882. Munich: Reinhardt, 1995.

Maillot, Alphonse, and André Lelièvre. *Les Psaumes: Traduction nouvelle et commentaire. 3. Psaumes 101–150 avec en appendice des Psaumes de Qumran*. Geneva: Labor et Fides, 1969.

Magne, Jean. "Recherches sur les Psaumes 151, 154 et 155." *RQ* 8 (1975) 503–7.

Mingana, Alphonse, and J. Rendel Harris. "Some Uncanonical Psalms: Introductory Note. Translation." *BJRL* 11 (1927) 327–498.

Meyer, Rudolf. "Die Septuaginta-Fassung von Psalm 151, 1–5, als Ergebnis einer dogmatischer Korrektur." In *Das Ferne und Nahe Wort: Festschrift für Leonhard Rost*, edited by Fritz Maass, 164–72. BZAW 105. Berlin: Töpelmann, 1967.

Noth, Martin. "Die fünf syrisch überlieferten apokryphen Psalmen." *ZAW* 48 (1930) 1–23.

Philonenko, Marc. "L'origine essénienne des cinq psaumes syriaques de David." *Sem* 9 (1959) 35–48.

Pigué, Stefan C. "The Syriac Apocryphal Psalms: Text, Texture, and Commentary." PhD diss., Southern Baptist Theological Seminary, 1988.

Ploeg, J. P. M. van der. "Un petit rouleau de psaumes apocryphes (11Q PsAp^a)." In *Tradition und Glaube: Das frühe Christentum in seiner Umelt. Festgabe*

für Karl Georg Kuhn zum 65. Geburtstag, edited by Gert Jeremias et al., 128-39. Göttingen: Vandenhoeck & Ruprecht, 1971.
Sachau, Eduard. *Verzeichniß der syrischen Handschriften der königlichen Bibliothek zu Berlin*, vol. 1. Berlin: Asher, 1899.
Sanders, James A. "The Qumran Psalms Scroll [11QPs[a]] Reviewed." In *On Language, Culture, and Religion: In Honor of Eugene A. Nida*, edited by Matthew Black and William A. Smalley, 79-99. Approaches to Semiotics 56. The Hague: Mouton, 1974.
Skehan, Patrick W. "Again the Syriac Apocryphal Psalms." *CBQ* 38 (1976) 143-58.
Strothman, Werner. *Wörterverzeichnis der apokryphen-deuterokanonischen Schriften des alten Testaments in der Peshitta*. GOFS 27. Wiesbaden: Harrassowitz, 1988.
Strugnell, John. "More Psalms of 'David.'" *CBQ* 27 (1965) 207-16.
Techen, L. "Syrisch-Hebräisches Glossar zu den Psalmen nach der Peschita." *ZAW* 17/1 (1897) 129-71.
Van Rooy, H. F. "The Marginal Notes to the Syriac Apocryphal Psalms in Manuscript 12T4." *VT* 48/4 (1998) 542-54.
———. "Die siriese apokriewe Psalms in die Manuskrip 12t4." *AT* 16/1 (1996) 107-27.
Vermes, Geza. "Apocryphal Psalms (I)." In *The Complete Dead Sea Scrolls in English*, 301-4. New York: Penguin, 1997.
Weber, Robert, et al., eds. *Biblia sacra: iuxta Vulgatam versionen*. Stuttgart: Deutsche Bibelgesellschaft, 2007.
Westermann, Claus. "Psalmen, syrische." *BHH* 3. Cols. 1522-23.
Wigtil, David N. "The Translation of Religious Texts in the Greco-Roman World." PhD diss., University of Minnesota, 1980.
Woude, A. S. van der. *Die fünf syrischen Psalmen*. JSHRZ 4.1-3. Gütersloh: Mohn, 1974.
Wright, William. "Some Apocryphal Psalms in Syriac." *Proceedings of the Society of Biblical Archaeology* 9 (1887-1888) 257-66.

BIBLIOGRAPHY

Psalm 151

Auffret, Pierre. "Structure littéraire et interprétation du Psaume 151 de la grotte XI de Qumrân." *RQ* 9 (1977-1978) 163-88..

Baumgarten, Joseph M. "Perek shirah, An Early Response to Psalm 151." *RQ* 9 (1978) 575-78.

Benson, Michael Eric. "Hasmoneans, Herodians, and Davidic Descent: Kings and Kingship in Post-Biblical Jewish Literature." PhD diss., New York University, 1996.

Brownlee, William Hugh. "The 11Q Counterpart to Psalm 151:1-5." *RQ* 4 (1963) 379-87.

———. "The Significance of 'David's Compositions.'" *RQ* 20 (1966) 569-74.

Bruyn, Joseph Jacobus de. "In Remembrance of God's Messianic Vessel—'Body' and 'Space' in Psalm 151." *Biblische Notizen* 168 (2016) 163-83.

Carmignac, Jean. "La forme poétique du psaume 151 de la grotte 11." *RQ* 4 (1963) 371-78.

———. "Nouvelles précisions sur le Psaume 151." *RQ* 8 (1972-1975) 593-97.

———. "Précisions sur le forme poétique du Psaume 151." *RQ* 5 (1964-1966) 249-52.

Collela, Pasquale. "Il testo ebraico del Salmo 151." *RivB* 14 (1966) 365-68.

Cross, Frank Moore. "David, Orpheus, and Psalm 151:3-4." *BASOR* 231 (1978) 69-71.

Debel, Hans. "Amalgamator or Faithful Translator? A Translation-Technical Assessment of Psalm 151." In *The Composition of the Book of Psalms*, edited by Erich Zenger, 443-61. BETL 238. Leuven: Peeters, 2010.

———. "'The Lord Looks at the Heart,' (1 Sam 16:7): 11QPs[a] as a 'Variant Literary Edition' of Ps 151 LXX." *RQ* 23 (2008) 459-73.

———. "De psalm die 'buiten het getal' valt: Psalm 151 in de Septuaginta en in de rollen van de Dode Zee." *Collationes* 40 (2010) 7-20.

Delcor, M. "Zum Psalter von Qumran." *BZ* 10 (1966) 15-29.

Dupont-Sommer, André. "David et Orphée." *Séance publique annuelle des cinq Académies, Lundi 26 octobre 1964*. Plaquette 20. Paris: Institut de France, 1964.

———. *Le mythe d'Orphée aux animmaux et ses prolegemente dans le Judaïsme Christianisme et l'Islam*. Academia Nazionale dei Lincei 214. Rome: Academia Nazionale dei Linzi, 1975.

———. "Notes quomraniennes sur 11QPsa xxii." *Sem* 15 (1965) 74-78.

———. "Le Psaume CLI dans *11QPsa* et le problème de son origine essénienne." *Sem* 14 (1964) 25-62.

———. "Le psaume hébreu extra-canonique (11QPsa, col. XXVIII)." *L'annuaire du College de France* 64 (1964-1965) 317-20.

Ebied, R.Y. "A Triglot Volume of the Epistle to the Laodiceans, Psalm 151 and Other Biblical Materials." *Bib* 47 (1966) 251-54.

Haran, M. "The Two Text-Forms of Psalm 151." *JJS* 39 (1988) 171-82.

Hoenig, Sidney B. "Review of *The Qumran Liturgical Psalms*." *JQR* 57 (1967) 327-32.
Hurvitz, Avi. "The Language and Date of Psalm 151 from Qumran." *Eretz Israel* 8 (1957) 82-87.
———. "The Post-Biblical Appelation, 'Master of All' (*Adon Hakkol*) and Its Appearance in Psalm 151 from Qumran." *Tarbiz* 34 (1965) 224-27.
Magne, Jean. "Orphisme, pythagorisme, essénisme dans le texte hébreu du Psaume 151." *RQ* 8 (1975) 508-47.
———. "Seigneur de l'Univers' ou David-Orphée? Défense de mon interpretation de Psaume 151." *RQ* 9 (1977-1978) 189-96.
———. "Les Textes grec et syriaque du Psaume 151." *RQ* 8 (1975) 548-64.
———. "Le verset des trios pierres dans la tradition du Psaume 151." *RQ* 8 (1975) 565-91.
Mancini, Renata. "Note sul salmo 151." *RSO* 65/1-2 (1991) 125-29.
Matsuda, I. "Three Apocryphal Hymns from 11QPsa." *Bungaku-Kenkyu* 76 (179) 81-104.
Meyer, Rudolf. "Die Septuaginta-Fassung von Psalm 151,1-5 als Ergebnis einer dogmatischen Korrektur." In *Das Ferne und Nahe Wort: Festschrift Leonhard Rost zur Vollendung seines 70. Lebenjahres am 30. November 1966*, edited by Fritz Maass, 164-72. BZAW 105. Berlin: Töpelmann, 1967.
Newsome, Carol A. "Psalm 151." In *Women's Bible Commentary*, edited by Carol A. Newsome and Sharon H. Ringe, 335-36. Louisville: Westminster John Knox, 1998.
Ovadia, Asher. "בית־הכנסת בעזה." *Qadmoniot* 1 (1968) 124-27.
Philonenko, Marc. "David et Orphée sur une mosaïque de Gaza." *RHPR* 47 (1967) 355-57.
———. "David humilis et simplex. L'interprétation essénienne d'un personage biblique et son iconographe." *CRAIBL* 121 (1977) 536-48.
———. "Prudence et le Psaume 151 ('Dittochaeon' XIX)." In *Le Psautier chez les Pères*, 291-96. Cahiers de Biblia Patristica 4. Strasbourg: Centre d'analyse et de documentation patristiques, 1994.
Ploeg, J. P. M. van der. "Fragments d'un manuscript des psaumes de Qumrân." *RB* 74 (1967) 408-12.
Rabinowitz, Isaac. "The Alleged Orphism of 11Q Pss 28, 3-12." *ZAW* 76 (1964) 193-200.
Sanders, James A. "A Multivalent Text: Psalm 151:3-4 Revisited." *Hebrew Annual Review* 8 (1984) 167-84.
———. "Ps. 151 in 11QPss." *ZAW* 75/1 (1963) 73-86.
Schneider, Heinrich. "Biblische Oden im syrohexaplarischen Psalter." *Bib* 40 (1959) 199-209.
Segal, M. H. "The Literary Development of Psalm 151: A New Look at the Septuagint Version." *Textus* 21 (2002) 159-74.
Sen, Felipe. "El Salmo 151 merece anadirse al Salterio como obra maestro." *CB* 29 (1972) 168-73.

BIBLIOGRAPHY

Silberman, Lou H. "Prophets/Angels: LXX and Qumran Psalm 151 and the Epistle to the Hebrews." In *Standing before God: Studies on Prayer in Scriptures and in Tradition with Essays in Honor of John M. Oesterreicher*, edited by Asher Finkel and Lawrence Frizzell, 91–101. New York: Ktav, 1981.

Sitarz, E., and Stefaniak, L. "Qumránski manuskrypt Psalmu 151 (11QPss)." *Znak* 133–34 (1965) 936–38.

Skehan, Patrick W. "Apocryphal Psalm 151." *CBQ* 25 (1963) 407–9.

Smit, E. J. "Ps 151 uit Septuaginta en Qumran." *Koers* 36 (1969) 246–57.

Smith, Mark S. "How to Write a Poem: The Case of Psalm 151 A (11QPsa 28,3–12)." In *The Hebrew of the Dead Sea Scrolls and Ben Sira: Proceedings of a Symposium Held at Leiden University, 11–14 December 1995*, edited by T. Muraoka and J. F. Elwolde, 182–208. STDJ 26. Leiden: Brill, 1997.

Smith, Morton. "Psalm 151, David, Jesus, and Orpheus [11QPsa]." *ZAW* 93 (1987) 247–53.

Spoer, Hans H. "Psalm 151." *ZAW* 28 (1908) 65–68.

Staalduine-Sulman, Eveline van, and G. W. Lorein. "CsD II, 4–IV, 9: A Song of David for Each Day." *Henoch* 31 (2009) 387–410.

Starcky, Jean. "Le psaume 151 des Septante retrouvé à Qumran." *MdB* 7 (1979) 8–10.

Stern, Henri. "Un nouvel Orphée-David dans une mosaïque de VIe siècle." *CRAIBL* 114 (1970) 63–79.

Storfjell, J. Bjørnar. "The Chiastic Structure of Psalm 151." *Andrews University Seminary Studies* 25 (1987) 97–106.

Strelcyn, Stefan. "Le psaume 151 dans la tradition éthiopienne." *JSS* 23 (1978) 316–29.

Strugnell John. "Notes on the Text and Transmission of the Apocryphal Psalms 151, 154 (= Syr. II.) and 155 (= Syr. III.)." *HTR* 59 (1966) 257–81.

Talmon, Shemaryahu. "Extra-Canonical Hebrew Psalms from Qumran—Psalm 151." In *The World of Qumran from Within: Collected Studies*, 244–72. Leiden: Brill, 1989.

Tronina, Antoni. "Psalm 151—Poetycki midrasz do dziejów Dawida." *RTK* 43/1 (1996) 81–87.

Tryjarski, Edward. "A Fragment of the Apocryphal Psalm 151 in its Armeno-Kipchak Version." *JSS* 28 (1983) 297–302.

Uffenheimer, Benjamin. "Psalm 151 from Qumran." *Molad* 22 (1964) 69–81.

Van Rooy, H. F. "Die verhouding van die siriese Psalm 151 tot die griekse en hebreeuse Weergawes." *SK* 18 (1997) 176–97.

Viaud, Gérard. "Le Psaume 151 dans la liturgie copte." *BIFAO* 67 (1969) 1–8.

Wigtil, David. N. "The Sequence of the Translations of Apocryphal Psalm 151." *RQ* 11 (1983) 401–7.

Witt, Andrew C. "David, the 'Ruler of the Sons of His Covenant' (מושל בבני בריתו): The Expansion of Psalm 151 in 11QPsa." *JESOT* 3 (2014) 77–97.

Psalm 152

Benson, Michael Eric. "Hasmoneans, Herodians, and Davidic Descent: Kings and Kingship in Post-Biblical Jewish Literature." PhD diss., New York University, 1996.

Van Rooy, H. F. "The Textual Traditions and Origin of Syriac Apocryphal Psalm 152." *JNSL* 21 (1995) 93–104.

Ufenheimer, Benjamin. "Psalms 152 and 153 from Qumran: Two More Apocryphal Psalms." *Molad* 22 (1964) 191–92, 328–42.

Bibliography

Psalm 153

Benson, Michael Eric. "Hasmoneans, Herodians, and Davidic Descent: Kings and Kingship in Post-Biblical Jewish Literature." PhD diss., New York University, 1996.

Morawe, Günter. "Vergleich des Aufbaus der Danklieder und hymnischen Bekenntnislieder (1QH) von Qumran mit dem Aufbau der Psalmen im Alten Testamen und im Spätjudentum." *RQ* 4 (1963–1964) 323–56.

Ufenheimer, Benjamin. "Psalms 152 and 153 from Qumran: Two More Apocryphal Psalms." *Molad* 22 (1964) 191–92, 328–42.

Van Rooy, H. F. "The Origin of Syriac Apocryphal Psalm 153." *JSem* 6 (1994) 97–109.

BIBLIOGRAPHY

Psalm 154

Auffret, Pierre. "Structure littéraire et interprétation de Psaume 154 de la grotte 11 de Qumrân." *RQ* 9 (1978) 163–88, 513–45.
Christ, Felix. "11QPsa XVIII." In *Jesus Sophia. Die Sophia-christologie bei den Synoptikern*, 39–42. ATANT 57. Zurich: Zwingli, 1970.
Delcor, M. "Zum Psalter von Qumran." *BZ* 10 (1966) 15–29.
Dupont-Sommer, André. "Explication de textes hébreux découverts à Qoumrân: The Psalms Scroll of Qumran Cave 11 (11QPsa)." *Annuaire du Collège de France* 66 (1966) 358–67.
Eshel, Esther, et al. "4Q448, 4QApocryphal Psalm and Prayer." In *Qumran Cave 4.VI: Poetical and Liturgical Texts, Part 1*, edited by Esther Eshel, et al, 403–25. DJD 11. Oxford: Clarendon, 1998.
———. "A Qumran Composition Containing Part of Ps. 154 and a Prayer for the Welfare of King Jonathan and His Kingdom." *IEJ* 42 (1992) 199–229.
———. "A Scroll from Qumran That Includes Parts of Psalm 154 and a Prayer for King Jonathan and His Kingdom." *Tarbiz* 6 (1991) 295–324.
Eshel, Hanan, and Esther Eshel. "4Q448, Psalm 154 (Syriac), Sirach 48:20, and 4QpIsaa." *JBL* 119 (2000) 645–59.
García Martínez, Florentino. "Salmos Apócrifos en Qumran." *EstBib* 40 (1982) 197–220.
Harrington, Daniel J. *Wisdom Texts from Qumran*. The Literature of the Dead Sea Scrolls. London: Routledge, 1996.
Hoenig, Sidney B. "The Qumran Liturgic Psalms." *JQR* 57 (1967) 327–32.
Juhás, Peter. "Žalm 154: Text a jeho kritické skúmanie." *Studia Biblica Slovaca* (2007) 35–53.
Kister, Menahem. "Qumran Corner: Notes on Some New Texts from Qumran." *JJS* 44/2 (1993) 280–90.
Lebram, Jürgen-Christian. "Die Theologie der späten Chokma und häretisches Judentum." *ZAW* 77 (1965) 202–11.
Lemaire, André. "Attestation textuelle et critique littéraire: 4Q448 col A. et Psalm 154." In *The Dead Sea Scrolls: Fifty Years After Their Discovery: Proceedings of the Jerusalem Congress, July 20–25, 1997*, edited by Lawrence H. Schiffman et al., 12–18. Jerusalem: Israel Exploration Society, 2000.
Lührmann, Dieter. "Ein Weiheitspsalm aus Qumran (11QPsa XVIII)." *ZAW* 80 (1968) 87–98.
Magne, Jean. "Le Psaume 154." *RQ* 9 (1977) 95–102.
———. "Le Psaume 155." *RQ* 9 (1977) 103–11.
Sanders, James A. "Psalm 154 Revisited." In *Biblische theologie und gesellschaftlicher Wandel: Für Norbert Lohfink SJ*, edited by Georg Braulik, et al., 296–306. Freiburg: Herder, 1993.
Sen, Felipe. "Traducción y commentario del Salmo 154, por primera vez en castellano." *CB* 29 (1972) 43–47.
Skehan, Patrick W. "Again the Syriac Apocryphal Psalms." *CBQ* 38 (1976) 143–58.

Van Rooy, H. F. "The Hebrew and Syriac Versions of Psalm 154." *JSem* 5 (1993) 97–109.

———. "Psalm 154:14 and the Relation between the Hebrew and Syriac Versions." *JBL* 116 (1997) 321–24.

Psalm 155

Auffret, Pierre. "Structure littéraire et interpretation de Psaume 155 de la grotte XI de Qumrân." *RQ* 9 (1978) 323–56.
Delcor, M. "Zum Psalter von Qumran." *BZ* 10 (1966) 21–28.
Dupont-Sommer, André. "Explication de textes hébreux découverts à Qoumrân: The Psalms Scroll of Qumran Cave 11 (11QPsa)." *Annuaire du Collège de France* 66 (1966) 358–67.
Eshel, Esther, et al. "4Q448, 4Q Apocryphal Psalm and Prayer." In *Qumran Cave 4.VI: Poetical and Liturgical Texts, Part 1*, edited by Esther Eshel, et al, 403–25. DJD 11. Oxford: Clarendon, 1998.
Eshel, Hanan, with Shlomit Kendi-Harel. "Psalm 155: An Acrostic Poem of Repentance from the Second Temple Period." In *Exploring the Dead Sea Scrolls: Archaeology and Literature of the Qumran Caves*, edited by Shani Tzoref and Barnea Levi Selavan, 226–56. JAJSup 18. Göttingen: Vandenhoeck & Ruprecht, 2015.
García Martínez, Florentino. "Salmos Apócrifos en Qumran." *EstBib* 40 (1982) 205–7.
Greenfield, Jonas C. "Two Notes on the Apocryphal Psalms." In *Sha'arei Talmon: Studies in the Bible, Qumran, and the Ancient Near East Presented to Shemaryahu Talmon*, edited by Michael Fishbane et al., 309–14. Winona Lake, IN: Eisenbrauns, 1992.
Hurwitz, Avi. "Observations on the Language of the Third Apocryphal Psalm from Qumrân (11QPs III)." *RQ* 5 (1965) 225.
Magne, Jean. "Psaume 154 et Psaume 155." *RQ* 9/1 (1977) 95–111.
———. "Le Psaume 155." *RQ* 9 (1977) 103–11.
Morawe, Günter. "Vergleich des Aufbaus der Danklieder und hymnischen Bekenntnislieder (1QH) von Qumran mit dem Aufbau der Psalmen im Alten Testament und im Spätjudentum." *RQ* 4 (1963–1964) 323–56.
Qimron, Elisha. "Some Remarks on the Apocryphal Psalm 155 (11QPsa Column 24)." *JSP* 10 (1992) 57–59.
Skehan, Patrick W. "Again the Syriac Apocryphal Psalms." *CBQ* 38 (1976) 143–58.
———. "A Broken Acrostic and Psalm 9." *CBQ* 27 (1965) 1–5.
Van Rooy, H. F. "Psalm 155: One, Two or Three Texts?" *RQ* 16 (1993) 109–22.

BIBLIOGRAPHY

Psalm 156 (MS RNL Antonin 798)

Bar-Ilan, Meir. "Non-Canonical Psalms from the Genizah." In *The Dead Sea Scrolls in Context: Integrating the Dead Sea Scrolls in the Study of Ancient Texts, Languages, and Cultures*, edited by Armin Lange et al., 2:693–718. 2 vols. VTSup 140/2. Leiden: Brill, 2011.

Charlesworth, James H. "Discovering Psalm 156 and Discerning Its Importance for Early Judaism and Christian Origins." In *Anatomies of the Gospels and Early Christianities*, edited by Elizabeth Struthers Malbon et al. BIS. Leiden: Brill, 2018 [in press].

Fleischer, Ezra. "Medieval Hebrew Poems in Biblical Style." *Te'uda* 7 (1991) 200–248.

Flusser, David, and Shemuel Safrai. "The Apocryphal Psalms of David." In *Judaism of the Second Temple Period*. Vol. 1, *Qumran and Apocalypticism*, 258–82. Translated by Azzan Yadin. Grand Rapids: Eerdmans, 2007.

———. "שירי דודי החיצוניים." *Te'uda* 2 (1982) 83–105.

Harkavy, A. E. "Prayers in the Style of the Songs of the Psalms by an Anonymous Person" (Heb.). *Ha-Goren: Abhandlungen über die Wissenschaft des Judenthums* 3 (1902) 82–85.

Lorein, G. W., and Eveline van Staalduine-Sulman, "A Song of David for Each Day: The Provenance of the Songs of David." *RQ* 85 (2005) 33–59.

Philonenko, Marc, and Alfred Marx. "Quatre 'Chants' Pseudo-Davidiques trouvés dans la gueniza du Caire et d'origine Esséno-Qoumrânienne." *Revue d'histoire et de philosophie Religieuses* 77 (1997) 385–406.

Stec, David M. *The Genizah Psalms: A Study of MS 798 of the Antonin Collection*. Cambridge Genizah Studies Series 5. Études sur le Judaïsme médiéval 57. Leiden: Brill, 2013.

BIBLIOGRAPHY

Psalms 151-155 and Qumran Hymns and Prayers

Beckwith, Roger T. "The Courses of the Levites and the Eccentric Psalms Scrolls from Qumran." *RQ* 11(1984) 499-524.

Charlesworth, James H., et al., eds. *Angelic Liturgy: Songs of the Sabbath Sacrifice*. PTSDSSP 4B. Tübingen: Mohr/Siebeck, 1999.

———. *Pseudepigraphic and Non-Masoretic Psalms and Prayers*. PTSDSSP 4A. Tübingen: Mohr/Siebeck, 1997.

Chazon, Esther G. "Psalms, Hymns, and Prayers." In *EncyDSS* 2:710-15.

———. "Prayers from Qumran and Their Historical Implications." *DSD* 1 (1994) 265-84.

———. "The Function of the Qumran Prayer Texts." In *The Dead Sea Scrolls: Fifty Years After Their Discovery*, edited by Lawrence H. Schiffman et al., 217-25. Jerusalem: Israel Exploration Society, 2000.

Chyutin, Michael. "The Redaction of the Qumranic and the Traditional Books of Psalms as a Calendar." *RQ* 16 (1994) 367-95.

Cook, Johann. "On the Relationship between 11QPsa and the Septuagint on the Basis of the Computerized Data Base (CAQP)." In *Septuagint, Scrolls, and Cognate Writings: Papers Presented to the International Symposium on the Septuagint and Its Relations to the Dead Sea Scrolls and Other Writings (Manchester, 1991)*, edited by George J. Brooke and Barnabas Lindars, 107-30. SBLSCS 33. Atlanta: Scholars, 1992.

Dupont-Sommer, André. "Le psaume hébreu extra-canonique (11QPsa, col. XXVIII)." *Annuaire du College de France* 64 (1964-1965) 317-20.

Fabry, Heinz-Josef. "11QPsa und die Kanonizität des Psalters." In *Freude an der Weisung des Herrn: Beiträge zur Theologie der Psalmen. Festgabe zum 70. Geburtstag von Heinrich Groß*, edited by Ernst Haag and Frank-Lothar Hossfeld, 45-67. SBB 13. Stuttgart, 1986.

Falk, Daniel K. "Prayer in the Qumran Texts." In *The Early Roman Period*, edited by William Horbury et al., 852-76. Cambridge History of Judaism 3. Cambridge: Cambridge University Press, 1999.

Farrell, Shannon Elizabeth. "Le rouleau 11QPsa et le psautier biblique: Une etude comparative." *LTP* 46/3 (1990) 353-68.

Fitzmyer, Joseph A. "Detailed Analysis of the Contents of 11QPsa." In *The Dead Sea Scrolls: Major Publications and Tools for Study*, 37-38. SBLSBS 8. Missoula: Scholars, 1975.

Flint, Peter W. "The '11QPsa Psalter' in the Dead Sea Scrolls, including the Preliminary Edition of 4QPse." In *The Quest for Context and Meaning: Studies in Biblical Intertextuality in Honor of James A. Sanders*, edited by Craig A. Evans and Shemaryahu Talmon, 173-96. BIS 28. Leiden: Brill, 1997.

———. "'Apocrypha,' Other Previously-Known Writings, and 'Pseudepigrapha' in the Dead Sea Scrolls." In *The Dead Sea Scrolls after Fifty Years: A Comprehensive Assessment*, edited by Peter W. Flint and James C. VanderKam, 2:24-66. 2 vols. Leiden: Brill, 1999.

———. "The Book of Psalms in Light of the Dead Sea Scrolls." *VT* 48 (1998) 453-72.

———. "The Contribution of the Cave 4 Psalms Scrolls to the Psalms Debate." *DSD* 5 (1998) 320-33.

———. *The Dead Sea Psalms Scrolls and the Book of Psalms*. STDJ 17. Leiden: Brill, 1997.

———. "Of Psalms and Psalters: James Sanders' Investigation of the Psalms Scroll." In *A Gift of God in Due Season: Essays on Scripture and Community in Honor of James A. Sanders*, edited by Richard D. Weis and David M. Carr, 65-83. JSOTSup 225. Sheffield: Sheffield Academic, 1996.

———. "Psalms, Book of: Apocryphal Psalms." In *EncyDSS* 2:708-10.

———. "The Psalters at Qumran and the Book of Psalms." PhD diss., University of Notre Dame, 1993.

Flusser, David. "Qumran and Jewish 'Apotropaic Prayers.'" In *Judaism and the Origins of Christianity*, 214-25. Jerusalem: Magnes, 1988.

García Martínez, Florentino. "Salmos apócrifos en Qumran." *EstBib* 40 (1982) 197-220.

García Martínez, Florentino, and Eibert J. C. Tigchelaar. *The Dead Sea Scrolls Study Edition*. 2 vols. Leiden: Brill, 1998.

———. "Psalms Manuscripts from Qumran Cave 11: A Preliminary Edition." *RQ* 17 (1996) 73-107.

Glück, J. J. "Nagid-Shepherd." *VT* 13 (1963) 144-50.

Goshen-Gottstein, Moshe H. "The Psalms Scroll (11QPs^a): A Problem of Canon and Text." *Textus* 5 (1966) 22-33.

Gurewicz, S. B. "Hebrew Apocryphal Psalms from Qumran." *AusBR* 15 (1967) 13-20.

Habermann, Abraham Meir. "שלושה מזמורים חיצויים ממדבר יהודה." *Beit Mikra: Journal for the Study of the Bible and Its World* 13 (1964) 3-9.

"Three New Non-Canonical Psalms from the Scroll Found in the Desert of Judah." *Molad* 2, 7 (1968) 94-98.

Haran, Menahem. "11QPs^a and the Canonical Book of Psalms." In *Minhah le-Nahum. Biblical and Other Studies Presented to Nahum M. Sarna in Honour of His 70th Birthday*, edited by Marc Brettler and Michael Fishbane, 193-201. JSOTSup 154. Sheffield: Sheffield Academic, 1993.

Hoenig, Sidney B. "The Dead Sea Psalms Scroll." *JQR* 58 (1967-1968) 162-63.

———. "The Qumran Liturgic Psalms." *JQR* 57 (1967) 327-32.

Homan, Martin J. "A Comparative Study of the Psalter in the Light of 11QPs^a." *WTJ* 40 (1978) 116-29.

Hurvitz, Avi. "The Language and Date of Psalm 151 from Qumran." *Eretz Israel* 8 (1957) 82-87.

———. "Observations from the Language of the Third Apocryphal Psalm from Qumran." *RQ* 5 (1965) 225-32.

———. "The Post-Biblical Epithet 'Master of All' (*Adon Hakkol*) and Its Appearance in Psalm 151 from Qumran." *Tarbiz* 34 (1965) 224-27.

———. "Psalms, Apocryphal." In *EncyJud* 13:1302-3.

Kraus, Hans-Joachim. *Psalms 1–59: A Commentary*. Translated by Hilton C. Oswald. Continental Commentaries. Minneapolis: Augsburg, 1988.

———. *Psalms 60–150: A Commentary*. Translated by Hilton C. Oswald. Continental Commentaries. Minneapolis: Augsburg, 1989.

———. *Theology of the Psalms*. Translated by Keith Crim. Continental Commentaries. Minneapolis: Augsburg, 1986.

Lehmann, Manfred R. "11QPs[a] and Ben Sira." *RQ* 11 (1982–1984) 239–51.

Moraldi, Luigi. "Dal Rotolo del Salmi (11QPs[a])." In *I Manoscritti di Qumrān*, 465–94. Classici delle religioni. Sezione seconda, La Religione ebraica. Turin: Unione Tipografico-Editrice Torinese, 1971.

Nitzan, Bilhah. *Qumran Prayer and Religious Poetry*. Translated by Jonathan Chipman. STDJ 12. Leiden: Brill, 1994.

Philonenko, Marc. "David et Orphée sur une mosaïque de Gaza." *RHPR* 47 (1967) 355–57.

———. "Une expression qumrânienne dans le Coran." In *Atti del terzo Congresso di Studi Arabi e Islamici: Ravello, 1966*, 553–56. Naples: Istituto Universitario Orientale, 1967.

———. "Une tradition essénienne dans le Coran." *RHR* 170 (1966) 143–57.

Polzin, Robert. "Notes on the Dating of the Non-Massoretic Psalms of 11QPs[a]." *HTR* 60 (1967) 468–76.

Puech, Émile. "Les Psaumes Davidiques du rituel d'exorcisme (11Q11)." In *Sapiential, Liturgical and Poetical Texts from Qumran*, edited by Daniel K. Falk et al., 160–81. STDJ 35. Leiden: Brill, 2000.

Qimron, Elisha. "The Psalms Scroll of Qumran—A Linguistic Study." *Lešonénu* 35 (1970) 99–116.

Sanders, James A. "Cave 11 Surprises and the Question of Canon." *McCQ* 21 (1968) 284–98.

———, ed. *The Dead Sea Psalms Scroll*. Ithaca: Cornell University Press, 1967.

———. "Palestinian Manuscripts 1947–1972." *JJS* 24 (1973) 74–83.

———. "Pre-Masoretic Psalter Texts." *CBQ* 27 (1965) 114–23.

———. "Psalms Scroll." In *EncyDSS* 2:715–17.

———. *The Psalms Scroll of Qumrân Cave 11 (11QPsa)*. DJD. Oxford: Clarendon, 1965.

———. "The Qumran Psalms Scroll (11QPsa) Reviewed." In *On Language, Culture, and Religion: In Honor of Eugene A. Nida*, edited by Matthew Black and William E. Smalley. Approaches to Semiotics 56. The Hague: Mouton, 1974.

———. "The Scroll of Psalms (11QPss) from Cave 11: A Preliminary Report." *BASOR* 165 (1962) 11–15.

———. "The Scrolls and the Canonical Process." In *The Dead Sea Scrolls after Fifty Years: A Comprehensive Assessment*, edited by Peter W. Flint et al., 2:1–23. 2 vols. Leiden: Brill, 1999.

———. "Two Non-Canonical Psalms in 11QPsa." *ZAW* 76 (1964) 58–74

———. "*Variorum* in the Psalms Scroll (11QPsa)." *HTR* 59 (1966) 83–94.

Schams, Christine. *Jewish Scribes in the Second-Temple Period*. JSOTSup 291. Sheffield: Sheffield Academic, 1998.

Schuller, Eileen M. "4Q380 and 4Q381: Non-Canonical Psalms from Qumran." In *The Dead Sea Scrolls: Forty Years of Research*, edited by Devorah Dimant, and Uriel Rappaport. Leiden: STJD 10. Brill, 1992.

———. *Non-Canonical Psalms from Qumran: Pseudepigraphic Collection*. HSS 28. Atlanta: Scholars, 1986.

———. "Prayer at Qumran." In *Prayer from Tobit to Qumran: Inaugural Conference of the ISDCL at Salzburg, Austria, 5–9 July 2003*, edited by Renate Egger-Wenzel and Jeremy Corley, 411–28. Deuterocanonical and Cognate Literature Yearbook 2004. Berlin: de Gruyter, 2004.

———. "Prayer, Hymnic, and Liturgical Texts from Qumran." In *The Community of the Renewed Covenant: The Notre Dame Symposium on the Dead Sea Scrolls*, edited by Eugene Ulrich and James VanderKam, 153–71. Christianity and Judaism in Antiquity 10. Notre Dame: University of Notre Dame Press, 1993.

Siegel, Jonathan P. "Final *Mem* in Medial Position and Medial *Mem* in Final Position in 11QPsa: Some Observations." *RQ* 7 (1969–1971) 126–30.

Sinclair, Lawrence A. "11QPsa—A Psalm Scroll from Qumran: Text and Canon." In *The Psalms and Other Studies on the Old Testament Presented to Joseph I. Hunt, Professor of Old Testament and Hebrew, Nashotah House Seminary, On His 70th Birthday*, edited by Jack C. Knight and Lawrence A. Sinclair, 109–15. Cincinnati: Forward Movement, 1990.

Skehan, Patrick W. "*Jubilees* and the Qumran Psalter." *CBQ* 37 (1975) 343–47.

———. "A Liturgical Complex in 11QPsa." *CBQ* 35 (1973) 195–205.

———. "Qumran and Old Testament Criticism." In *Qumrân: sa piété, sa théologie et som milieu*, edited by M. Delcor, 163–72. BETL 46. Paris: Duculot, 1978.

Skehan, Patrick W., et al. "The Cave 4 Psalms Scrolls." In *Qumran Cave 4: XI: Psalms to Chronicles*, edited by Eugene Ulrich, et al., 7–170. DJD 16. Oxford: Clarendon, 2000.

Skehan, Patrick W., et al. "A Scroll Containing 'Biblical' and 'Apocryphal' Psalms: A Preliminary Edition of 4QPsf." *CBQ* 60 (1998) 267–82.

Smith, Mark S. "How to Write a Poem: The Case of a Psalm 151 A (11QPsa 28,3–12)." In *The Hebrew of the Dead Sea Scrolls and Ben Sira: Proceedings of a Symposium Held at Leiden University, 11–14 December 1995*, edited by T. Muraoka and J. F. Elwolde. 182–208. STDJ 26. Leiden: Brill, 1997.

Smith, Morton. "Psalm 151, David, Jesus, and Orpheus [11QPsa]." *ZAW* 93 (1987) 247–53.

Starcky, Jean. "Psaumes apocryphes de la grotte 4 de Qumrân (4QPsf vii–x)." *RB* 73 (1966) 353–71.

Talmon, Shemaryahu. "The Emergence of Institutional Prayer in Light of Qumran Literatuere." In *The World of Qumran from Within: Collected Essays*, 200–243. Leiden: Brill, 1989.

———. "Hebrew and Apocryphal Psalms from Qumran." *Tarbiz* 35 (1965–1966) 214–34.

———. "Pisqah Be'emsa' Pasuq and 11QPsa." *Textus* 5 (1966) 11–22.

Ulrich, Eugene. "Multiple Literary Editions: Reflections toward a Theory of the History of the Biblical Text." In *Current Research and Technological Developments on the Dead Sea Scrolls: Conference on the Texts from the Judean Desert, Jerusalem, 30 April 1995*, edited by Donald W. Parry and Stephen D. Ricks, 99–101. STDJ 20. Leiden: Brill, 1996.

———. "The Septuagint Manuscripts from Qumran: A Reappraisal of Their Value." In *The Septuagint and Its Relations to the Dead Sea Scrolls and Other Writings*, edited by George J. Brooke and Barnabas Lindars, 49–80. SBLSCS 33. Atlanta: Scholars, 1992.

Wacholder, Ben Zion. "David's Eschatological Psalter: 11Q Psalms." *HUCA* 59 (1988) 23–72.

Wilson, Gerald H. *The Editing of the Hebrew Psalter*. SBLDS 76. Chico, CA: Scholars, 1985.

———. "The Qumran Psalms Manuscript and the Consecutive Arrangement of Psalms in the Hebrew Psalter." *CBQ* 45 (1983) 377–88.

———. "The Qumran Psalms Scroll Reconsidered: Analysis of the Debate." *CBQ* 47 (1985) 624–42.

———. "The Qumran "Psalms Scroll" (11QPSa) and the Canonical Psalter: A Comparison of Editorial Shaping." *CBQ* 59 (1997) 448–64.

Wolters, Al. "The Tetragrammaton in the Psalms Scroll." *Textus* 18 (1995) 87–99.

Yadin, Yigael. "Another Fragment (E) of the Psalms Scrolls from Qumran Cave 11." *Textus* 5 (1966) 1–10.

———. "Psalms from a Qumran Cave." *Molad* 22 (1964) 643–65.

Author Index

Astren, Fred, 74n42
Auffret, Pierre, 22n68

Baars, Willem, 1n2, 10n18
Bar-Ilan, Meir, 57, 57n2, 58n3, 61n10, 63, 63n19, 63n20, 64, 64n22, 70, 70n31, 71n34, 71n35, 73n38, 73n39, 76, 83, 83n12
Bock, Darrell L., 91n17
Braun, Oscar, 74n45
Burrows, Millar, 74, 75n46

Carmel, Alex, 73n38
Carmignac, Jean, 4n12
Charlesworth, James H., 1n2, 2n3, 3n8, 4n9, 8n17, 15n45, 16n47, 28n3, 65n23, 70n33, 78n1, 78n2, 80n7, 91n17, 92n19, 93n20, 99n2, 101n1
Cross, Frank Moore, 3, 3n6, 16n46

Delcor, M., 16n47
Dobbs-Allsopp, F. W., 1n1, 5, 5n13, 6n15
Dunn, James D. G., 54n241
Dupont-Sommer, André, 16n47

Eissfeldt, Otto, 74, 75n46
Engel, Edna, 65n23
Erder, Yoram, 74n42
Esler, Philip F., 86n14
Evans, Craig A., 54n240
Even-Shoshan, A., 30n31, 31n38,

Fallon, Francis T., 80n8
Field, Frederick, 74n44
Fleischer, Ezra, 58n3, 63, 63n15, 71n34
Flint, Peter W., 68, 68n29
Flusser, David, 37n99, 38n109, 39n118, 48n218, 57, 58, 58n3, 59, 59n7, 60, 61, 62, 62n12, 62n14, 64, 66, 66n24, 67, 69, 69n30, 70, 70n32, 71n35, 79, 79n3, 83n11, 93, 93n21,

Gieschen, Charles A., 92n18,
Goren, Haim, 73n38

Haran, Menahem, 63, 63n16,
Harkavy, A. E., 62, 62n13, 89, 89n16,
Harrington, Daniel J., 81n9
Hurtado, Larry W., 54n241
Hurvitz, Avi, 16n46

Author Index

Jastrow, Marcus A., 11n23

Kahle, Paul E., 73n40
Katsh, Abraham Isaac, 73n37
Knauf, Ernst Axel, 54n238, 54n239
Kraus, Hans-Joachim, 1n1
Kugel, James L., 1n1

Lee, Samuel, 10n18
Loke, Andrew Ter Ern, 55n241
Lorein, G. W., 58n5, 63, 63n18, 64
Lowth, Robert, 5, 5n14

Magne, Jean, 2n5, 4n12, 22n68
Marx, Alfred, 37n94, 43n158, 48n217, 48n218, 63, 63n17, 64, 93, 93n22
McDonald, Lee Martin, 72n36
Mendenhall, George E., 54n238
Mercati, Giovanni, 74n43
Milik, J. T., 75n46
Miller, Eric, 55n241
Miller, Patrick D., 1n1
Mishor, Mordechai, 65n23

Philonenko, Marc, 16n47, 37n94, 48n218, 63, 63n17, 64, 93, 93n22
Pigué, Stanley C., 2n4, 3n7
Polzin, Robert, 16n46
Pouilly, Jean, 16n48

Reibel, David A., 5n14
Reif, Stefan C., 74n42

Safrai, Samuel, 48n218, 57, 58, 58n3, 59, 59n7, 60, 61, 62, 62n12, 62n14, 64, 66, 66n24, 67, 69, 69n30, 70, 70n32, 71n35, 79, 79n3, 83n11, 93, 93n21
Sanders, James A., 1n2, 2n3, 2n4, 4n12, 6n16, 11n19, 15n45, 16n47, 17n50, 18n59
Seow, C. L., 39n120
Skehan, Patrick W., 16n46, 17n49, 22n68
Smith, Morton, 54n241
Staalduine-Sulman, Eveline van, 58n5, 63, 63n18, 64
Stec, David M., 37n94, 43n158, 48n217, 48n218, 50n235, 59, 59n6, 60, 63, 64, 64n21, 64n22, 68, 68n27, 80n6
Stegemann, Harmut, 73n40
Strugnell, John, 2n5, 4n12, 6n16, 21n66

Talmon, Shemaryahu, 61, 61n11
Toorn, Karel van der, 51n237

Welch, John W., 12n36
Wernberg-Møller, Preben, 16n48
Westermann, Claus, 1n1
Wieder, Naphtali, 74n42
Wilson, Gerald H., 1n1

Yardeni, Ada, 58, 58n4

Scripture, Qumran Scrolls, Pseudepigrapha, and Other Ancient Sources Index

Hebrew Bible / Old Testament

Genesis

	32n45, 58
1	29n13
6	90
18:7	37n102
25:13	35n74, 54
30:13	97
36:35	54

Exodus

2–4	54
15:11	31n35
15:26	83
18	54
24:17	40n137

Leviticus

15:28	37n95
16:19–20	84

Numbers

25	54
27:11	45n181

31	54

Deuteronomy

	71n35
6:4	47n209
23:10–15	39n125
27:15–26	61
33:29	97

1 Samuel

	7, 13, 43n163
2	43n163
2:7–8	43n163
16:6–13	7
17	8–10
17:33–36	13

2 Samuel

	43n163
7	81
7:14	36n92
7:16	43n169
7:19–29	31n41
12:30	33n59
22	43n163
22:3	49n221
23:1–7	81
23:2–3	82
23:2	50n235
23:5	48n215

Ancient Sources Index

1 Kings
6:1 — 82
7:21 — 92

1 Chronicles — 31n41, 45n185
12:18 — 50n234
13:5–8 — 39n120
13:8 — 39n123, 45n187
14:3 — 44n172
16:7 — 32n45
16:9 — 45n187, 79, 79n4
16:13–17 — 48n215
16:13 — 31n41
16:33 — 44n179
16:36 — 36n93
17:4 — 31n41
17:7 — 31n41
17:12 — 43n169
17:13 — 36n92
17:24 — 31n41
17:25 — 31n41
17:26 — 31n41
17:27 — 31n41
29:10 — 36n92

Ezra — 29n16

Nehemiah — 29n16

Job
12:10 — 45n190

Proverbs
10:25 — 92
28:14 — 98
29:18 — 98

Psalms
1–2 — 52
1:1 — 86, 97
9:9 — 29n13
9:13 — 47n204, 79
10:15 — 32n49
11:5 — 28n6
17:36–38 — 3
18:1 — 82
20 — 51n237
21:6 — 46n199
22 — 21
23 — 37n100
24:1 — 38n111, 46n197, 80
26:8 — 41n139
27:4 — 80
28:6 — 97n1
28:7 — 50n234
31:22 — 97n1
32:1–2 — 98
33:12 — 98
40:4 — 30n24, 80
40:5 — 35n82, 98
41:2 — 98
41:13 — 61
41:14 — 59, 98
42 — 52
44–49 — 52
44:23 — 37n99, 63n19
49:17 — 82
51:6[4] — 50n233
51:10 — 37n102
58:12 — 44n179
59:17 — 34n65
65:5 — 98
68:6 — 48n212
69:16 — 11n23
71:16 — 38n113
72 — 52
72:2 — 29n13
72:18–20 — 42n157, 60
72:19 — 61
72:20 — 52

Ancient Sources Index

75:2[1]	40n135	119	62, 96
75:11	49n222	119:1	98
80:13[12]	33n53, 80	119:2	98
81:3	39n123	119:72	41n143
84	41	120–134	52
84:1–2	64, 79	120:5	35n74, 54, 80
84:2	41n139	121:3	35n76
84:5	98	124	52
84:6	98	126:2–3	44n173
86:11	42n148	127	52
89	79	128:1	98
89:2	31n41	131	52
89:4	31n41	133	52
89:16	98	137:7–9	43n163
89:21	31n41	145:12	38n113
89:28	34n69, 79	147:3	37n105
89:40	48n215	150:2	38n113
89:52	61	151–155	ix, ch. 1, 52, 55, 56, 71, 76, 78, 95
90	52		
91	76		
94:2	44n179	151	61, 72, 80
94:12	98	151 A	44n178, 72
95:2	39n124	151 A v. 4c	80
96:13	29n13	151 A v. 11	80
97:9	39n127	151 B	72
98:9	29n13	154	52, 56, 72, 78
100:2	30n22	155	52, 56, 57, 72, 78
103:1	82, 97n1		
103:2	97n1	155:9–13	51
103:20	97n1		
103:21	97n1	Isaiah	
103:22	97n1		47n209, 68, 78, 80, 87, 89
105:2	45n186, 45n187, 79	2:18	40n130, 80
106	61	2:20	40n130, 80
106:3	98	3:10	49n228
106:24	34n62, 80	5	29n20
106:48	48n216, 59, 60, 61, 79	5:5	33n53, 80
		9:3	34n70
112–119	52	11:4	29n13
112:1	98	21:1	80
118:22	33n55, 33n57, 80, 92, 93, 93n20	21:16–17	35n74, 54
		40:21	32n45
		42–46	87

Ancient Sources Index

Isaiah (*continued*)
42:6	38n106, 38n107, 67
43:10	42n152
49:6	38n106, 38n107, 67, 80
51:3	39n123
51:5	32n49
51:9	32n49
52:10	32n51, 80
53:1	32n49
53:11	16
58:12	33n54
59	89
60:22	32n44

Jeremiah
2:10	54
2:14	49n228
17:10	49n228
32:19	49n228
48:25	32n49

Ezekiel
5:15	44n175
21:8–9	28n6
27:21	35n74, 54
36:23	34n64, 35n77

Hosea	68

Joel
2:20–21	44n175

Micha
	68
7:4	37n105

Nahum	68

Habakkuk	68

Zephaniah	68

Zechariah
11:4	37n100
11:7	37n100

∼

New Testament

Matthew	85, 86, 88, 99
5	99
5:1–12	85, 88–89, 99
11:6	85, 99
13:16	85, 99
16:16–17	89
16:17	85, 99
21:42	92
24:46	85, 99

Mark
8:29–30	89
8:33	89
12:10	92
14:36	42n150
Luke	85, 86, 88, 99
1:32–33	91
1:45	85, 99
1:52	43n163
6	99
6:20–23	85, 99
6:20–26	88
7:23	85, 99
10:23	85, 99
11:27–28	85, 99
12:37–38	85, 99
12:43	85, 99
14:14–15	85, 99
20:17	92
23:29	85, 99
John	85
13:17	85, 99
20:29	85, 99

Ancient Sources Index

Acts	
2:29–30	50n235
2:30	82
4:11	93

Romans	
4:7–8	85, 99
11:26	89
14:22	85, 99

Galatians	
2:9	33n52, 92

Ephesians	
1:5	29n19

1 Timothy	
3:15	92

Hebrews	92, 93
1:1–4	92
1:4	90, 92

James	85, 99
1:12	85, 99
1:25	85, 99

1 Peter	
2:7	93

Revelation	85
1:3	85, 99
3:12	92
10:1	92
14:13	85, 99
16:15	85, 99
19:9	85, 99
20:6	85, 99
22:7	85, 99
22:14	85, 99

Apocryphal/Deuterocanonical

Sirach	45n185, 85, 99
14:20–27	85, 98
25:8–9	85, 98
26:1	85, 98
36:10	32n44
49:8	40n136

1 Maccabees	
13:49	66
14:11	66

4 Maccabees	85
7:15	85, 98

~

Qumran Scrolls

Prayers for Festivals (1Q34, 1Q34^{bis}; 4Q507–509)	96

Qumran *Psalms Scroll* (11QPs^a, 11Q5)	3, 6n16, 16, 16n46, 21, 22, 56, 57, 66, 67, 68, 71, 72, 78, 80n7, 82
24.4–5	42n150
27.2–11	82n10
27.2	38n106, 67
27.4	67
27.5	80n7
27.11	50n235, 67
col. 28	7
28.3–14	72
28.11	80

~

Ancient Sources Index

Rule of the Community (1QS)		Thanksgiving Hymns (1QH, 1QHª)	
	17n52, 29n14, 84		33n61, 38n114, 85
col. 1	18n56	2.43	17
1.20	61	3.19–23	16
col. 2	18n56	5.13–14	17
2.2	18n55	col. 6	18n56
2.10	61	6.13–15	85, 98
2.18	61	7.35	28n11
col. 3	18n56, 82, 84	col. 11	18n56
3.2	18n55	11.10–14	16
3.9	18n55	col. 12	18n56
3.13–4.26	28n6, 29n14	12.39	28n6
4.22	17, 18n55	col. 13	18n56
col. 5	18n56	col. 14	18n56
col. 6	18n56	col. 16	18n56, 29n20
6.8–7.25	16	col. 18	18n56
6.17	18n55	col. 19	18n56
col. 7	18n56		
col. 8	18n56	Words of the Lights (4Q504–506; 4QDib Hamª⁻ᶜ)	96
8.1	18n55		
8.10	18n55	1QIsaª	40n130
8.14	36n86	1QM	85
8.18	18n55	13.2	85, 98
8.20	18n55		
8.21	18n55	1QpHab	
col. 9	18n56	col. 7	32n44, 38n114
9.2	18n55	1Q16	68, 81
9.5	18n55		
9.6	18n55	4QBeatitudes (4Q525)	62, 85, 86, 88, 98, 99
9.8	18n55		
9.9	18n55		
9.19	18n55	4QEnᵍ	
col. 10	18n56	1.4	29
		4QŠirŠabb	16
Self-Glorification Hymn	31n37, 34n65, 34n68, 47n203, 54, 55n241, 67, 90, 92	4Q171	68, 81
		4Q173	68, 81
		4Q185	85
		frgs. 1–2 2.8	85, 98
		frgs. 1–2 2.13–14	85, 98
		4Q216	
		2.15	44n175

4Q286	76	*1 Enoch*	37n100, 71n34, 90
frg. 7a col. 2b–d line 1	61	1–36	16
frg. 7a col. 2b–d line 5	61	58:2	86, 98
frg. 7a col. 2b–d line 6	61	89:19	37n101
frg. 7a col. 2b–d line 10	61	90:25	37n101
4Q503	76	93	29n20
11QMelchizedek	90		

∽

Pseudepigrapha and Other Ancient Sources

Acts of Paul
5–6   99

Amidah
14   32n48

Antiquities of the Jews, Josephus
14.77   65, 85
13.215   66

Apocalypse of Abraham   16

Aramaic Testament of Levi   57, 65, 66, 73, 77

Babylonian Talmud
Berakot 61b   99

Hagîgâ 12b   33n52, 99

Homa 86a   99

Sotah 48b   50n235, 68, 82

3 Baruch   16

Bereshith Rabba
54   30n31

2 Enoch   16, 86, 88, 99
42:6–14   86, 98
52:1–15   86, 98

Gospel of Thomas   86
13   90
54   86, 99
66   93
68–69a   86, 99
69b   86, 99

Guide for the Perplexed, Maimonides
3:43   37n95

Hesiod   97

Hexapla, Origen   74

History of the Rechabites   85, 99n2
14:5   85, 99

Hymn of the Pearl   4n9

Jewish Tombstone   99

Joseph and Aseneth   86

Liber Antiquitatum Biblicarum
51:6   38n107

Mishnah   31n38, 56

Rosh Ha-Shanah 3   83

Ancient Sources Index

Naturalis Historia, Pliny the Elder
5.11[12]	54
65	54

Odes of Solomon
11:18–19	29n20
24:1	32n45

Odyssey, Homer
5	97
7	97
24	97
191–92	97

Parables of Enoch — 91, 91n17

Petosiris — 97

Pseudo-Philo — 16, 43n165, 81, 86
60:2–3	81n9

Psalms of Solomon — 65, 84
2:1	65
14:2	29n20

Ramses II — 97

Satyricon, Petronius
94.1	97

Targum of Isaiah
52:13	32n46

Targum on the Psalms
14	54
18	54
18:1	50n235, 68, 82
49:12	50n235
49:16	54
49:17	68, 82
103	54
103:1	50n235, 68, 82

Testament of Abraham — 16

Testament of Job — 16, 86

Testament of Judah — 67

Wars of the Jews, Josephus
13.214	66

Zohar
3:97a–b	37n95

www.ingramcontent.com/pod-product-compliance
Lightning Source LLC
Chambersburg PA
CBHW022122160426
43197CB00009B/1119